YOU
WERE MADE
for
MORE

Walk boldly. Rise confidently.

Live the life God designed for you

DR. MONA L. BRAWLEY

DEDICATION

To my mother, **Betty**,

Whose life whispered courage
and whose love taught me "more."

You learned boldly,
served faithfully,
and loved generously;
from taking classes in a pandemic
to calling church members as a deacon
even days before your final hospital stay.

You showed me that growth has no age,
dreams have no deadline,
and hope always finds its way forward.

Your "Mimisms" still echo through our family,
and your signature blessing:
"Have a blessed forever,"
continues to rest over us
like a gentle benediction.

I miss you deeply,
but your legacy lives inside every step
I take on the life God designed for me.

Thank You, Lord,
for the gift of being her daughter.

ENDORSEMENTS FOR YOU WERE MADE FOR MORE

Some books inform, and then there are books that awaken your soul. "You Were Made for More" is a divine invitation. Literally an altar in written form. Through her transparent testimony and powerful insight, Dr. Mona Brawley calls every woman to silence the lies of "not enough" and step boldly into the abundance of who God created her to be.

Her words breathe restoration. Each Selah moment feels like The Father whispering, "Daughter, breathe... You were made for **More**." Not more performance, not more striving, but more of your authentic presence. Dr. Mona writes with the heart of a teacher, the courage of a prophet, and the tenderness of a sister who knows what it means to rise from the ashes with purpose.

This book is more than a message. It's a movement of healing, identity, and divine awakening. Let these pages remind you: you are seen, you are chosen, and you are already enough.

— **Dr. Darlene "McCoy" Jackson**
National Radio Host + Author + Artist + Faith Leader

"You Were Made for More" is a powerful reminder that with God, we are already equipped for greatness. Dr. Mona Brawley masterfully leads readers on a heartfelt journey from identity to legacy—helping them heal, dream, and walk boldly in their divine purpose.

— **Dr. Sherry Gaither**, Author, Speaker, and
Transformational Life Coach

You Were Made for More by Dr. Mona L. Brawley is a warm, encouraging, and biblically grounded invitation for women to rediscover their identity in Christ and live with clarity and purpose. Through Scripture, personal reflection, and practical guidance, Dr. Brawley helps readers confront the lies that limit them, receive healing and wholeness, and embrace the calling God has placed on their lives. Each chapter includes thoughtful reflection prompts and prayers that support genuine spiritual growth. This book is both inspiring and practical— ideal for women's ministries, mentorship settings, or personal devotional study—and it reminds every reader that the "more" we are made for is found not in striving, but in surrendering to God's loving design. It is a refreshing and empowering invitation to live healed, whole, grounded in identity, and committed to leaving a legacy of faith.

— **Pastor K. Charlene Williams, Adjunct Professor**
North Central University

You Were Made for More is a beautiful invitation to rediscover who God created you to be. Dr. Mona Brawley writes with grace, strength, and a tenderness shaped by a life of deep faith. Her words challenge, encourage, and guide women back to intimacy with Christ—the true source of purpose and abundance. This book will bless you, strengthen you, and lead you into the "More" God has already prepared for you.

— **Dr. Nina Bronner,** *Word of Faith Family Worship Cathedral*

My friend Dr. Mona Brawley's book "You Were Made for More" finds its origin in the book of origins especially in the creation narrative in Genesis 1:27 "So God created man in his own image, in the image of God created he him; male and female created he them." Mona reminds us that as God's image bearers we were built for more – just like God is limitless so are we. You will read, grow and embrace this message of More.

*— **Brenda C. Chand, DMin,** Co-Founder Dream Releaser Coaching and author of The Professional Coaching Handbook*

TABLE OF CONTENTS

FOREWORD

There are moments in a woman's life when her heart begins to stir with whispers she can no longer silence. A holy restlessness. A sacred ache. It sounds like longing, but it is actually an invitation— an echo from Heaven reminding her that she was never created to live small, shadowed, or half-awake. This book you hold in your hands is born from that whisper.

Dr. Mona Brawley has extended her ear to the heartbeat of God and returned with a message for every woman who has ever paused mid-stride and wondered, "Lord… is there more?" Not more noise. Not more hustle. Not more expectations stacked on already-tired shoulders. But more life. More purpose. More identity. More of Him.

In these pages, Mona becomes both midwife and mentor, gently guiding you through the contractions of self-doubt, the labor pains of comparison, the quiet suffocations of "not enough," and the subtle lies that slither into a woman's soul until she forgets who she is and Whose she is.

Like Eve, we are all familiar with the hiss of that ancient question— "Did God really say…?" Oh, how cunning the enemy is. He doesn't roar; he whispers. He doesn't snatch; he suggests. Yet Mona pulls back the veil with such tender clarity, revealing that the battle for identity is not new—but neither is the victory Christ has secured for us.

What I love most about Mona's writing is how she makes truth personal. She leads us to Scripture the way a friend leads another to a quiet well—inviting us not to sip timidly but to drink deeply. Her stories carry the weight of authenticity, the kind of transparency that refuses to glamorize the journey. She is refreshingly honest about her own wrestling matches—with insecurity, with calling, with the subtle temptation to shrink back. And yet, her testimony becomes a lantern for anyone stumbling through the fog of self-doubt.

This is not a book that merely inspires; it equips. Each chapter is a divine invitation to pause, reflect, and realign. To breathe again. To come home to the truth of your design. To reclaim what has always been yours—your identity, your voice, your purpose, your belonging.

Mona reminds us that God is not the God of "barely enough." He is the God of overflow, abundance, and More. And the way into that More is not through striving, but through surrender; not by performing, but by remembering; not by fixing yourself, but by allowing Truth to fix your gaze on the One who formed you.

Whether you are a weary leader, a hidden servant, a silent struggler, or a woman whose smile masks a storm—this book is an answered prayer. A gentle hand on the shoulder. A holy nudge toward the life God always intended. You will leave these pages not only knowing who you are, but walking in it… with grace, confidence, and renewed fire.

So, exhale. Slow your pace. Open your heart. Settle into the sacred pauses scattered throughout this journey. For in those Selah moments, Heaven leans close.

And perhaps, if you listen carefully, you'll hear it too—the whisper that has been pursuing you since Eden:

"Daughter… You were made for More."

Michelle McKinney Hammond, Bestselling Author of "The Power of Being a Woman" and "The Diva Principle"

INTRODUCTION
The Invitation to *More* Life

There comes a moment in every woman's life when her soul whispers a question she can no longer ignore: *Is this it? Is this all I was made for?*

You may not say the question out loud. Maybe you've learned to smile through it, to keep showing up, to carry the weight of everyone else's needs while quietly wondering when someone will notice yours. But late at night, when the noise fades and the mask slips, that ache still hums beneath the surface—the longing for *more*.

Not more things.
Not more noise.
But more life.
More meaning.
More peace.
More purpose.
More of God.

I know that ache. I've lived it.

For me, the questioning wasn't born in a storm; it came in a classroom. Lesson plans piled high on my desk, my two youngest children curled up asleep on beanbags in the corner, and exhaustion pressing me into my chair like quicksand. I loved my students, my family, and my ministry, but I felt swallowed up by the ordinary. Grateful, yet empty. Fulfilled, yet unfulfilled.

That day, I whispered the question that became the catalyst for everything that followed: *Lord, am I made for more than this?*

That question became an altar. And the answer came softly, but unmistakably: *"Yes—you were made for More."*

The Ache That Awakens

The ache for More is not a sign of rebellion; it's a sign of divine invitation. It's how Heaven stirs the soul awake.

You were never meant to live a life of quiet discontent or spiritual survival. You were made to flourish, to live a life that reflects God's abundance, not scarcity. Jesus said, "I have come that they may have life, and have it to the full" (John 10:10 NIV). That's not a metaphor. It's a mission statement.

> *"The ache for More is not a sign of rebellion; it's a sign of divine invitation. It's how Heaven stirs the soul awake."*

The More Life is not about adding activities; it's about awakening identity. It's about remembering who you are and *Whose* you are, and allowing that truth to shape how you see, love, serve, and live.

This book is an invitation to step into the More Life, a journey of rediscovery, healing, and purpose. Each chapter unfolds like a pathway toward wholeness, guiding you through the places where your faith, purpose, and calling intersect. It follows the M.O.R.E. framework—a transformational pathway that mirrors how God awakens, heals, forms, and sends us:

M — Manifest God's Original Design
O — Overcome What Holds You Back
R — Radiate God's Purpose & Image
E — Embrace the More Life

And because the word manifest has been misused in culture, I want you to hear this clearly:

When Scripture speaks of something being "made manifest," it means revealed, made visible, brought forth, expressed outwardly. *In the KJV and NKJV translations, these truths appear explicitly in John 2:11, 2 Corinthians 4:10–11, and Romans 8:19.*

So here, manifest does not mean "create your own reality." It simply means: **to allow the identity God designed within you to become visible in your life.** That is deeply biblical—and beautifully freeing.

- **Chapter 1** reminds you that you are not disqualified by your "not enoughs." When you meet God's More, miracles happen.
- **Chapter 2** helps you throw off the labels, lies, and comparisons that keep you bound. You'll learn to see yourself not through the world's filters but through the mirror of God's truth.
- **Chapter 3** invites you to trust again, to step out of the boat like Peter, even when fear whispers louder than faith.
- **Chapter 4** echoes the voice of Jesus asking, "Do you want to be made whole?" It's about healing not just the body, but the heart and soul.
- **Chapter 5** reminds you that God uses what's already in your hand. Your everyday gifts—your creativity, your compassion, your calling—are divine tools for His purpose.

- **Chapter 6** opens your eyes to vision, enabling you to dream again, to believe in the impossible, and to walk by faith, not by sight.
- **Chapter 7** helps you make sense of the scars and seasons that shaped you as you discover beauty in the ashes and purpose in the pain.
- **Chapter 8** reminds you that you cannot do life alone. God calls you to community—to lift up, pray for, and hold each other in the hard times.
- **Chapter 9** calls you to legacy, to live the More Life not for applause or accomplishment, but so that generations after you will know Christ through your impact. This is more than a book—it's a roadmap, a mirror, and a movement. Each page is an invitation to rise higher, go deeper, and live freer.

Making the Most of the *More* Life

Before you begin, pause and breathe.

Selah.

That's a word you'll see often in these pages.

In Hebrew, *Selah* means "to pause and reflect"—to stop and listen for what God is saying. It is the sacred pause, the holy space between revelation and response, when we quiet our hearts to hear Heaven's whisper. Throughout this book, you will find these moments marked as *Selah Reflections*. Each one invites you to:

> *"This is more than a book—it's a roadmap, a mirror, and a movement."*

- *Pause* and rest your soul in God's presence.
- *Reflect* on what He is revealing through Scripture.

- *Record* what He is stirring in your heart.
- *Rejoice* in His faithfulness and promises.

You'll also find:

- *Topical Prayers* at the close of each section to center your heart in worship.
- *Pause and Reflect Questions* to help you listen to what the Holy Spirit is saying personally to you.
- *Journal Spaces* for capturing your thoughts, revelations, and testimonies along the way.

These Selah moments are not detours—they are sacred resting places. They are where transformation deepens and truth becomes personal. So, slow down. Don't rush through the pages. Let each truth sink in. Let the Word wash over you. Let the Holy Spirit meet you in the quiet.

And when you pause long enough to listen, you may just hear the whisper again: *"You were made for More."*

The God of *More*

God has always been a God of More. From the beginning, His creation overflowed with abundance, seas teeming with life, skies filled with stars, and ground bursting with fruit. And even now, He whispers to weary hearts, "See, I am doing a new thing!" (Isaiah 43:19).

But before He gives us the More, He often calls us to trust Him in the "less."

Before He multiplies, He asks us to surrender.

Before He fills, He empties.

Before He sends, He heals.

The More Life is not found in striving but in surrender. It's in the whispered "yes," the one that says, "Lord, I trust You with what's in my hand, even when it doesn't feel like enough."

Like Moses with his staff.

Like the widow with her oil.

Like Peter with his net.

Like Mary with her alabaster jar.

God never asks for what you don't have. He multiplies what you do.

The Power of "Yes"

Every chapter of this journey begins with a yes.

A yes to healing.

A yes to faith.

A yes to surrender.

> *"God never asks for what you don't have. He multiplies what you do."*

A yes to community.

A yes to purpose.

Your yes is the key that unlocks your next season. Your yes is your offering of trust in the hands of a faithful God. That's how my journey began.

A yes in a classroom.

A yes in a hospital room.

A yes at an altar.

A yes that led from the ordinary to the extraordinary—not because I was extraordinary, but because I said yes to an extraordinary God.

This book is for the woman who's tired of surviving and ready to start thriving.

For the woman who's poured out for everyone else but quietly wonders if her time has passed.

For the woman who's waiting for permission to dream again.

For the woman who loves Jesus deeply but still wrestles with doubt, fear, or shame.

It's for the weary leader.

The mother who feels unseen.

The daughter who's still healing.

The believer who's hungry for more of God.

It's for *you*.

The Invitation

So here it is—your invitation to the More Life.

Not a life free of struggle, but a life full of meaning.

Not a life of perfection, but one of presence.

Not a life of striving, but a life of surrender.

The More Life is waiting, not at the end of your strength, but at the beginning of His. So, take a deep breath. Quiet your heart. And let these pages remind you that the same God who spoke, "Let there be light" still speaks to the darkness in you and says, "Rise."

Because you were never meant to live small.

You were never meant to live bound.

You were never meant to live empty.

You were made for More.

Selah: The Invitation to *More*

"I have come that they may have life, and have it to the full" John 10:10.

There is a whisper that awakens the soul, a quiet reminder that you were made for More. Not more busyness or more burden, but more life. The ache for More is not a sign of discontent; it is an invitation from Heaven to come closer.

God is not asking you to strive harder. He is inviting you to breathe deeper. To stop measuring your worth by what you do, and to rest in who He is. This journey begins not with a plan, but with a pause—a heart turned toward the One who gives life abundantly.

Take a moment to still your heart and receive this truth: The More you long for has always been found in His presence. And as you begin, ask yourself: *Who might God be calling me to bring along on this journey of More?*

Pause & Reflect

- Where do I sense God inviting me into a deeper experience of His life and love?
- What does "life to the full" mean to me in this season?
- Who do I need to take along this journey with me?

Prayer of Gratitude

Lord, awaken my heart to the fullness of life You've promised.

Quiet the striving within me, and teach me to rest in Your grace.

Fill me with Your presence until overflow becomes my norm. Amen.

M — MANIFEST GOD'S ORIGINAL DESIGN

Awaken and embody the identity God crafted in you from the beginning

"For those God foreknew he also predestined to be conformed to the image of his Son."
ROMANS 8:29 (NIV)

CHAPTER 1

"Did God Really Say?"

Identity Secured in Christ

"Did God really say…?" (Genesis 3:1)

That one question slithered into Eden like a serpent's hiss, and it hasn't stopped echoing through history since. The enemy's first strategy was not force, but suggestion. He didn't need chains, shackles, or weapons; all he needed was a whisper that seeded doubt. That whisper questioned God's word, twisted His intentions, and planted suspicion about His goodness.

Eve wasn't just tempted with fruit. She was tempted to believe she lacked something, that God was holding out on her, that His love and provision weren't enough.

That same whisper follows us today. It shows up in our mirrors, in our social feeds, in the quiet places of our thoughts: *Am I sure God said that about me? Am I sure I've been chosen? Am I sure I'm enough?*

It doesn't take much to recognize how familiar that hiss feels. We see it in every advertisement that tells us to "fix" ourselves. Every algorithm that highlights what we don't have. Every cultural voice that insists we're either too much or never enough. The battlefield of identity may look different now than it did in Eden, but the question is the same: *Did God really say?*

Every battle for identity is really a battle over whether you'll settle for less than God's promise or step into the More Life He created you for.

My Battle With "Not Enough"

I know that whisper well.

When I first stepped into ministry, I carried with me a catalog of insecurities. My height made me feel overlooked, my weight made me feel unworthy, and being a woman in a space often dominated by men made me feel out of place. Add to that an unconventional path into leadership, and the inner narrative sounded something like this: *You don't look the part. You don't fit the mold. You'll never be taken seriously.*

> "Every battle for identity is really a battle over whether you'll settle for less than God's promise or step into the More Life He created you for."

It wasn't just one voice; it was like a chorus of doubts that played on repeat. I showed up in pulpits and classrooms with the Word of God burning in my heart, but shame pressed down on me, heavy like fog. Fear whispered, *Shrink back.* Comparison said, *Blend in.* My own thoughts told me I wasn't qualified.

And yet, God had already spoken something else over me.

Long before I ever held a microphone, He said, "[You are] fearfully and wonderfully made" (Psalm 139:14).

Long before I earned degrees or titles, He proclaimed, "Before I formed you in the womb I knew you, before you were born I set you apart" (Jeremiah 1:5).

Long before the opinions of others tried to box me in, He declared, "For we are God's handiwork, created in Christ Jesus to do good works, which God prepared in advance for us to do" (Ephesians 2:10).

But in those early years, the lies often felt louder than the truth.

Identity Theft: Then and Now

Even if we haven't experienced it ourselves, we're familiar with the term *identity theft*. Someone steals your personal information, runs up debt in your name, and leaves you to clean up the mess. Identity theft is a crime that leaves people feeling violated, angry, and unsure who they really are in the eyes of the world.

That's exactly what the enemy did in Eden—and what he still tries to do today. He whispers lies, hoping we'll trade away our God-given identity for something counterfeit. He tries to run up debt in our name—shame, fear, and regret—but he never has the authority to rewrite what God has spoken.

Identity theft didn't start with stolen credit cards. It started with a stolen word: *Did God really say?*

The Anatomy of a Lie

If the enemy had a playbook, page one would read: *Start with a question.*

It was subtle, almost harmless. No accusations, no thunderbolts. Just a nudge of curiosity, a seed of doubt planted in the soil of Eve's mind. That's how deception works; it doesn't storm the gates; it slips through the cracks.

> "Identity theft didn't start with stolen credit cards. It started with a stolen word."

Jesus described the devil plainly: "He was a murderer from the beginning, not holding to the truth, for there is no truth in him. When he lies, he speaks his native language, for he is a liar and the father of lies" (John 8:44).

Satan doesn't invent new tactics. He doesn't need to, because the old ones still work. Every lie follows the same pattern:

- *Begin with a question.* Sow confusion, which causes us to second-guess God's Word.
- *Distort God's character.* Paint Him as restrictive, stingy, or unkind.
- *Attack your identity.* Suggest that we're lacking, incomplete, or forgotten.

Think about the last time you wrestled with insecurity. Didn't it sound familiar? *Are you sure you're called? Are you sure you belong here? Are you sure God loves you?* The script hasn't changed since Eden.

Eve: The First Target of Identity Confusion

When the serpent approached Eve, she already had everything she needed. She was walking with God in the cool of the day. She was perfectly designed, fully known, deeply loved. Yet the enemy made her feel as though something essential was missing: "For God knows that when you eat from it your eyes will be opened, and you will be like God, knowing good and evil" (Genesis 3:5).

The irony? Eve was already made in God's image (see Genesis 1:27). She already reflected His likeness. But the lie whispered that she wasn't enough as she was.

That's the same trick the Enemy pulls on us today. He tells the stay-at-home mom her work is insignificant. He tells the single woman she's incomplete without a partner. He tells the young leader she doesn't have the right look, the right voice, or the right résumé. He tells the seasoned believer her time has passed.

And if we're being honest here, sometimes we listen.

Eve's story is not just ancient history; it's a mirror. We see ourselves in her hesitation, in her curiosity, in her decision to reach for something outside of what God has already promised.

The Social Media Lie
If Eden had an Instagram feed, the serpent might have scrolled through it with Eve, pointing at filtered images of women who seemed more radiant, more confident, more successful. He would have whispered, "See? You're missing something."

Today, we don't need a talking serpent. We have algorithms that serve up a steady diet of comparison. One moment you're celebrating the life God gave you, and the next you're wondering why your life doesn't look like hers.

The serpent's whisper didn't die in the garden. It just got a Wi-Fi upgrade.

Whispers of God
Here's the thing: The enemy has his whispers, but God has His Word.

In the seasons when I felt the weight of *not enough* pressing down on my chest, God sent encouragers who spoke truth over me. They weren't always the people I expected, and sometimes they delivered just a simple word at the right moment. But their voices became lifelines.

I remember one Sunday, after a service where I had preached my heart out, I sat down thinking, *that wasn't good enough. I stumbled.*

I missed it. But before the self-criticism could settle in, a young woman approached me with tears streaming down her face. She said, "Pastor, that word changed my life today. God used you to speak directly to me."

Her words were a gentle rebuke from the Lord. While I had been measuring myself by performance, He reminded me that it was never about perfection; it was about obedience.

It was in moments like these that God began to interrupt the Enemy's lies with His unshakable truth, and the Scriptures that had once felt distant became deeply personal:

> "Before I formed you in the womb I knew you, before you were born I set you apart" (Jeremiah 1:5).

> "For we are God's handiwork, created in Christ Jesus to do good works, which God prepared in advance for us to do" (Ephesians 2:10).

> "I praise you because I am fearfully and wonderfully made; your works are wonderful, I know that full well" (Psalm 139:14).

These weren't just words on a page—they were declarations of identity. They reminded me that my worth wasn't up for debate and my calling wasn't up for grabs. The One who made me had already decided who I was.

And here's the truth: If He did it for me, He will do it for you.

> "It was never about perfection; it was about obedience."

Exposing the Common Lies About Identity

The Enemy is predictable, and he's not using any new material. His lies may take different forms, but the root is always the same: an attack on who God says you are.

- *Lie #1: You're not enough.*
  "My grace is sufficient for you, for my power is made perfect in weakness" (2 Corinthians 12:9).

- *Lie #2: You're too much.*
  "For we are to God the pleasing aroma of Christ among those who are being saved and those who are perishing" (2 Corinthians 2:15).

- *Lie #3: You'll never change.*
  "Therefore, if anyone is in Christ, the new creation has come: The old has gone, the new is here!" (2 Corinthians 5:17).

- *Lie #4: Your past disqualifies you.*
  "Therefore, there is now no condemnation for those who are in Christ Jesus" (Romans 8:1).

- *Lie #5: You must earn God's love.*
  "For he chose us in him before the creation of the world to be holy and blameless in his sight. In love he predestined us..." (Ephesians 1:4–5).

Securing Identity in Christ

The good news is this: Your identity is not fragile, even if it feels like it. It is not hanging by the thread of your performance or other people's opinions. Your identity is secured in Christ, sealed by the Spirit, and spoken over you by the Father:

> *"My worth wasn't up for debate and my calling wasn't up for grabs."*

"Yet to all who did receive him, to those who believed in his name, he gave the right to become children of God" (John 1:12).

"The Spirit himself testifies with our spirit that we are God's children. Now if we are children, then we are heirs—heirs of God and co-heirs with Christ" (Romans 8:16–17).

You are not just barely included in God's family; you are written into His will as an heir. That means your belonging is not conditional. A child does not knock at the door of her father's house, wondering if she's welcome. She walks right in because she knows who she is—his beloved and welcome daughter.

A Daily Battle Plan for Identity

If the serpent's whisper is daily, then your defense must be daily too. Here are four helpful steps for establishing a daily battle plan that helps you become more secure in your identity as one of God's beloved children:

1. *Recognize the lie.* Pause when a thought arises. Ask: *Does this align with God's Word?*
2. *Replace the lie with truth.* Speak Scripture out loud.
3. *Rest in Christ.* Lean into His finished work, not your own striving.
4. *Repeat God's Word daily.* Over time, the Enemy's lies will lose power as your heart becomes fluent in God's language.

A Prayer of Identity

Father, thank You that my identity is secure in You. I silence every lie that says I am not enough, too much, or unworthy. I declare that I am fearfully and wonderfully made, chosen, loved, and called. Help me to walk today in the truth of who You say I am. In Jesus' name, Amen.

Closing Invitation

The serpent is still whispering, but you don't have to listen. The Father's voice is louder, clearer, and truer. He calls you His beloved. He calls you His child. He calls you *enough*.

As you move forward, remember this: The question in Eden was never really about fruit. It was about identity. And the same is true for us today. The enemy will always try to make us doubt who we are and Whose we are. But the battle is already won.

Step into the More Life, not by doing more, but by believing more deeply what God has already spoken over you. As you settle into His truth, another question may arise: *If God already said it, why do we still believe the lies?*

Selah: Remember Who You Are

"Then God said, 'Let us make mankind in our image, in our likeness'" (Genesis 1:26).

Before the serpent whispered a single lie, God had already spoken the truth: "You are made in My image." Every lie that has followed since has been an attempt to make us forget that truth.

The enemy still whispers, "Did God really say...?" hoping you'll question what Heaven already declared. But God's voice has not changed. You are fearfully and wonderfully made. You are chosen, known, and loved. You don't have to earn your identity; it was settled before your first breath.

Take a moment to quiet every competing voice. Let the truth of who you are in

> "The serpent is still whispering, but you don't have to listen. The Father's voice is louder, clearer, and truer. He calls you His beloved. He calls you His child. He calls you enough."

Christ rise louder than the lies. Breathe in His affirmation. Breathe out the doubt. Let this be the moment you remember who you've always been—His child.

And as you walk forward, ask yourself: *Who do I need to take along on this journey of remembering? Can I take the hand of a sister, daughter, or friend who's forgotten her worth too?*

Pause & Reflect
- Where have I believed the whispers of "not enough"?
- What truth from God's Word do I need to reclaim today?
- Who in my life needs to be reminded of her identity in Christ?

Write honestly. Pray deeply. Let His presence steady you as you reflect.

A Prayer of Identity
Father, thank You that my identity is secure in You.

Silence every voice that speaks against what You have said.

Let Your truth settle deep in my heart and overflow into my words, my work, and my worship.

Remind me daily that I am Yours, made in Your image, loved beyond measure.

Amen.

Action Step: A Visible Declaration of Who You Are
Write your name in bold letters, and underneath it, declare three truths from Scripture about who God says you are. Post it on your mirror or journal cover as a daily reminder: *I am chosen. I am loved. I am enough in Christ.*

CHAPTER 2
"Who Told You That?"
Victory Over Lies & Hindrances

After Adam and Eve ate the fruit and hid themselves, God called out to them with a question that still pierces the soul: "And he said, 'Who told you that you were naked?'" (Genesis 3:11).

God already knew what had happened in Eden. He wasn't confused, nor was He seeking information. His question wasn't about exposure but about origin. Whose voice had they believed? And who had the *authority* to rename what God had called good?

It was the serpent's whisper. A counterfeit voice. A lie that twisted truth until God's beloved children saw themselves through shame instead of glory. And God, in His tenderness, asked the question that He still asks us today: "Who told you that?"

Who told you that you were unworthy?

Who told you that you were *too much* or *not enough*?

Who told you that your past defines you, or that your future is hopeless?

If it wasn't God, then it isn't true.

My Story: Learning Lies Through Friendship

Some of the earliest lies I carried about myself didn't come from teachers, sermons, or even loud accusations. They crept in quietly through my family dynamics and childhood friendships.

I was the youngest in my family. I had one brother who was just eighteen months older, and we were close. We often played together with his friends. My other siblings were much older: a brother eight years older, a sister nine years older, another sister ten years older, and my oldest brother eleven years older. My two eldest siblings weren't raised with me, so although I loved them, I didn't experience daily closeness with them as a child.

My sister Denise was brilliant, a genius-level scholar who graduated high school at fifteen, went to college at sixteen, and graduated at nineteen. We shared a room until she left for university when I was only seven. I admired her deeply and felt safe when she was around, but once she left, the house felt different. Suddenly, I didn't have a female figure close enough in age to share my everyday girlhood struggles with. Denise visited less frequently as the years went on, and I quietly learned to carry more by myself.

Around that time, my best friend, Candace, moved away. She had been my anchor. When she left, I felt exposed, vulnerable, and unmoored. And right in that gap, new girls moved onto my street.

At first, I just wanted to belong. But soon, I was pulled into a cycle of whispers, manipulation, and rejection. The new girls talked about me behind my back. They tried to sabotage my friendship with Candace when she came back on weekends to visit her grandmother.

I didn't know how to deal with this situation. I was shy, and I was afraid of being left out. So, I stayed quiet, even when their words cut deep. The more I tried to hold on, the unhappier I became. Their friendship was toxic, but I didn't realize it then.

Everything came to a head in the fourth grade. One afternoon, I had a vision from God—a glimpse of what was about to happen. I saw the girls' plan to jump me. When it unfolded, I was ready. I didn't even know where my strength came from, but after weeks of avoiding them, that day I stood up for myself.

The first time a fight nearly happened, my mother intervened, calling me inside before I understood what was going on. That spared me, but it didn't resolve the problem. I stayed close to home, trying to avoid the girls. Then one afternoon, I forgot. I wandered too far up the road, and the leader confronted me. This time, I fought back. And for the first time, I realized I wasn't powerless.

And yet, even in that moment of strength, I didn't hold on to it. When the leader of the girls came back later, offering her toxic friendship once again, I accepted. And I slipped into the same unhealthy cycle because I didn't yet recognize my worth. I hadn't yet seen my voice or my strength.

I remember praying as a child, desperate prayers whispered at night: *Lord, please move these girls away from me.* And God answered. The very next year, the leader's family moved off our street.

Years later, when I confronted her as a young woman, she surprised me with an apology. She confessed that she'd thought I had everything—that my family had money, that my home life was perfect. She admitted she had mocked me and even talked about my mother out of jealousy.

Her words stunned me. All those years of insecurity and bullying had been rooted in perception, not truth. She had labeled me privileged. I had labeled myself unwanted and unworthy. She looked at me and saw someone to envy. I looked at myself and saw someone desperate to be accepted.

That's the deceptive nature of lies. They rarely align with reality. They slip in through absence, through pain, through misunderstanding, and they stick like labels.

Even then, God's question was hovering over my life: *"Who told you that?"*

Naomi: From *Pleasant* to *Bitter*

Naomi's story is a vivid picture of how pain can rename us. Once called Naomi, a name meaning "pleasant," she returned to Bethlehem after losing her husband and both of her sons. The grief was so deep, the loss so unbearable, that when the women of Bethlehem greeted her by name, she stopped them: "Don't call me Naomi," she told them. "Call me Mara, because the Almighty has made my life very bitter" (Ruth 1:20).

In her despair, Naomi gave herself a new name: *Mara*, meaning "bitter." This was not the name God gave her. This was the name her pain gave her.

Isn't that what suffering tries to do to us? It tries to rename us. Divorce calls us *unworthy*. Failure calls us *not enough*. Grief calls us *broken*. But those names are lies. They may describe what we feel, but they do not define who we are.

When lies rename you, they try to cut you off from the More Life God has promised. But God's truth restores your identity and calls you back to the abundance you were created for.

The Hindrances That Keep Us Bound

Naomi's story shows how pain can rename us. Many of us carry names and labels God never gave us because we're lugging around burdens we were never meant to bear. I often picture it like trying to run a race with a suitcase in each hand. You might move forward, but every step is heavy, awkward, and exhausting. Imagine running like that for miles. You could still cross the finish line, but you'd be worn out long before you got there.

> "When lies rename you, they try to cut you off from the More Life God has promised."

That's what these hindrances are like: unnecessary suitcases weighing us down. Each one is filled with a different lie. And the longer we carry them, the more normal the weight feels, until we forget what freedom is supposed to feel like.

The writer of Hebrews urges us: "Therefore, since we are surrounded by such a great cloud of witnesses, let us throw off everything that hinders and the sin that so easily entangles" (Hebrews 12:1).

Notice it doesn't say "manage your baggage." It says throw it off. Lay it down. Refuse to carry what Christ already bore at the cross. Now, let's open these suitcases together and explore what's in them.

Fear: The Suitcase of "What Ifs"

Fear paralyzes. It keeps us staring at possibilities instead of stepping into promises. It sounds like: *What if I fail? What if they reject me? What if I'm not ready?* This suitcase rattles with imagined disasters, filled with worst-case scenarios that rarely happen. And yet fear convinces us it's safer to stay stuck than risk moving forward.

Every "what if" that fear whispers is meant to silence the truth of who we are in Christ. But Scripture draws a clear line between the lies of fear and the reality of our spiritual inheritance: "For the Spirit God gave us does not make us timid, but gives us power, love and self-discipline" (2 Timothy 1:7).

This verse reminds us that fear isn't part of our divine luggage; it's an uninvited weight we were never meant to carry. God has already packed for us what we truly need for the journey ahead: power to act in faith, love to quiet insecurity, and discipline to keep moving even when the road feels uncertain. It's time to unzip that suitcase of "what ifs," lay every fear before Him, and travel light in the confidence of His Spirit.

Shame: The Suitcase of Rocks

Shame doesn't just say, "You made a mistake." It hisses, "You *are* a mistake." Adam and Eve hid from God because shame distorted their identity. They covered themselves with fig leaves, convinced they were no longer worthy of God's presence. Shame is like a suitcase filled with rocks, each one with labels like *mistake, failure, not enough*. No wonder it feels so heavy.

But even when we hide, God still seeks us. His love calls us out of the shadows and invites us to see ourselves through His eyes. The psalmist reminds us of this liberating truth: "Those who look to him are radiant; their faces are never covered with shame" (Psalm 34:5).

When we dare to lift our eyes toward Him, the weight of shame begins to crumble. His light exposes not our flaws, but His grace at work within us. The rocks we once carried—our regrets, our self-condemnation, our past—are replaced with reminders of who we truly are: redeemed, beloved, and radiant in His presence. The only covering we need is His righteousness, not the fig leaves of our own striving.

Procrastination: The Suitcase of Excuses

Sometimes the enemy doesn't need to stop us outright; he just needs to *delay* us. And so he puts excuses in our mind: *I'll forgive later. I'll obey tomorrow. I'll step out when I'm ready.* But *later* rarely comes.

The suitcase of procrastination is stuffed with excuses, weighing us down with "someday." But the truth is, delayed obedience is still disobedience. Every time we tell ourselves "not yet," we miss the miracle that's waiting on the other side of our yes. Scripture reminds us that putting off what we know is right isn't harmless hesitation—it's sin that stifles our growth and dulls our sensitivity to God's voice: "If anyone, then, knows the good they ought to do and doesn't do it, it is sin for them" (James 4:17).

God invites us to unpack the suitcase of excuses and trade procrastination for partnership with His timing. The Holy Spirit doesn't rush us in panic, but He does nudge us toward action. Each small step of obedience today creates momentum for tomorrow's breakthroughs. When we choose to act now, in faith rather than fear, we discover that God has already gone before us, preparing the way and providing the strength we need to move forward.

Perfectionism: The Suitcase of Fragile Glass

Perfectionism tells us that if it isn't flawless, it isn't worth doing. It's like carrying a suitcase packed with fragile glass. You move carefully, terrified of dropping something, afraid of making a mistake. It whispers: "Don't share your gift until it's polished. Don't lead until you're an expert."

But perfectionism is a thief disguised as excellence. It convinces us that waiting until everything feels "just right" is wisdom, when in reality it's fear in disguise. Scripture exposes this trap and calls us back to faith-filled action: "Whoever watches the wind will not plant; whoever looks at the clouds will not reap" (Ecclesiastes 11:4).

If we keep waiting for perfect conditions, we'll miss the harvest God has already prepared. The truth is, God doesn't ask for perfection; He asks for obedience. Seeds don't have to be flawless to grow; they just need to be sown. When we offer Him our willingness instead of our perfection, He multiplies it into something far greater than we could ever achieve on our own. So unpack that suitcase of "not yet," and trust that His grace covers what your striving cannot.

Performance: The Suitcase of Trophies

Performance ties identity to accomplishments, applause, or the approval of others. This suitcase looks impressive on the outside—it's stuffed with trophies, medals, résumés—but it's exhausting to carry. The danger? When the performance ends, so does your sense of worth.

We live in a culture that measures value by what we *do* rather than who we *are*. But the gospel flips that completely. Jesus reminds us that our worth isn't earned through effort; it's received through relationship. When the crowds asked Him what work they must do to please God, His answer was simple yet deeply freeing: "Then they asked him, 'What must we do to do the works God requires?' Jesus answered, 'The work of God is this: to believe in the one he has sent'" (John 6:28–29).

Belief—not performance—is the starting point of a life that pleases God. He isn't after our perfection or productivity; He's after our hearts. When we learn to rest in His love, we realize that we don't have to *do* more to be accepted. We simply need to *be* who He created us to be. So, set down that suitcase of approval. Your identity is not in what you produce but in whose you are. The applause of heaven is already yours.

Comparison: The Suitcase of Mirrors

Comparison is like a suitcase lined with mirrors. Everywhere you look, you're measuring yourself against someone else. You either feel inferior (*She's so much better than me*) or superior (*At least I'm not like her*). Either way, the focus isn't on God; it's on the reflection.

Comparison is a quiet thief; it robs joy, distorts purpose, and shifts our gaze from the Creator to His creations. Paul warned the church about this trap, reminding us that our standard isn't each other but Christ Himself: "When they measure themselves by themselves and compare themselves with themselves, they are not wise" (2 Corinthians 10:12).

When we live through the lens of comparison, we miss the beauty of our own divine assignment. God didn't call you to run someone else's race or carry their gifts—He called you to walk faithfully in your own lane. The mirror of comparison magnifies insecurity, but the mirror of God's Word reflects truth: You are fearfully and wonderfully made, designed with a purpose that no one else can fulfill. So, close that mirrored suitcase, fix your eyes on Him, and walk confidently in the reflection of His grace, not the distortions of your own comparisons.

Suppression: The Suitcase Duct-Taped Shut

Suppression silences the gifts and voice God has given you. This suitcase is duct-taped shut, stuffed with buried dreams, silenced stories, and unused talents. It's dead weight that was never meant to be carried.

When we suppress what God has placed within us, we dim the very light He intends to shine through us. Sometimes it's fear, rejection, or past wounds that convince us to stay quiet—but God's design was never for His children to live hidden. Jesus reminds us of this truth in the Sermon on the Mount: "You are the light of the world. A town built on a hill cannot be hidden" (Matthew 5:14).

Your light was meant to shine, not shrink. Every gift, story, and talent He's placed in you carries the imprint of His glory. Suppression may feel safe, but it slowly suffocates purpose. When you dare to unzip that sealed suitcase and let your light break through, you give others permission to do the same. The world doesn't need a quieter version of you—it needs the God-breathed brilliance within you to rise and radiate for His glory.

Every suitcase looks different, but the root is the same: the Enemy's lie. Fear whispers you're not enough. Shame insists you're unworthy. Procrastination says you have time, while perfectionism convinces you everything must be flawless. Performance ties your worth to applause, comparison to others' reflection, and suppression to silence. Different labels—same lie. Each one begins with a false word spoken over your heart, designed to make you forget who you are and Whose you are.

But here's the hope: You don't have to carry these suitcases anymore. The One who carried the weight of the cross invites you to lay yours down. Jesus' invitation still stands for every weary soul: "Come to me, all you who are weary and burdened, and I will give you rest" (Matthew 11:28).

When you set down these suitcases at His feet, you make room for what He's always wanted you to hold: His peace instead of pressure, His grace instead of guilt, and His purpose instead of pretense. Rest isn't found in striving to be more; it's found in surrendering to the

One who already is *more than enough*. The journey toward freedom begins when you stop packing lies and start carrying truth.

The Turning Point: Breaking Agreement with the Lie

There comes a moment in every believer's journey when identifying the lie is no longer enough. We must break the *agreement* we made with it. Some agreements formed quietly over years, others in a single moment of pain—but every lie we accepted became a silent contract shaping our identity. Yet God never co-signed it.

Scripture gives us a clear path forward:

"We demolish arguments and every pretension that sets itself up against the knowledge of God, and we take captive every thought to make it obedient to Christ." 2 Corinthians 10:5

This is spiritual authority in action. It is the moment the contract gets torn.

To break the lie's power:

1. **Confront the lie as a spiritual intruder**—something that trespassed where it had no right to be.
2. **Renounce it aloud**, breaking agreement and taking the thought captive in obedience to Christ.
3. **Replace it with a God-given identity statement** rooted in His Word.
4. **Build a daily practice** that reinforces truth and strengthens your renewed mind.
5. **Invite accountability**, letting someone trustworthy stand with you.
6. **Take one bold action** that reflects the truth God declared and rejects the lie completely.

Transformation doesn't begin when you *recognize* the lie. It begins when you *refuse* to live under its authority another day.

An Invitation to Freedom in Christ

Every suitcase looks different, but the root is the same: the Enemy's lie. Each lie echoes the same deception that began in the garden of Eden: *God is holding out on you.* Each suitcase weighs you down with the burden of proving, earning, or hiding. But Jesus came to break that pattern once and for all.

Having a relationship with Jesus is what makes the More Life possible, because *He* is the "More" your soul has been searching for all along. Without Him, the battle for

> "Transformation doesn't begin when you recognize the lie. It begins when you refuse to live under its authority."

identity feels endless: always striving, never arriving. But in Him, your identity is secure, your worth is settled, and your purpose is redeemed.

The ache for More that's been stirring since the introduction—the longing that's been pulling you toward meaning, healing, and wholeness—is really an ache for *Him.* Jesus extends an invitation that dismantles every lie and offers rest to every weary heart: "Come unto me, all ye that labour and are heavy laden, and I will give you rest" (Matthew 11:28 KJV).

And He doesn't stop there. He declares the kind of life He came to bring: one overflowing with abundance, peace, and purpose: "The thief cometh not, but for to steal, and to kill, and to destroy: I am come that they might have life, and that they might have it more abundantly" (John 10:10 KJV).

That's the *More Life!* It is not a life built on perfection or performance; it is anchored in grace and filled with the presence of Christ Himself. When you come to Him, you're not just laying down heavy suitcases—you're exchanging them for freedom.

If you've never taken that step of bringing everything to Christ, the invitation is open now. Right where you are, you can pray a simple but life-changing prayer of surrender:

> *Lord Jesus, I admit I need You. I repent of my sins and turn to You. I want to live a life that pleases You. I believe You died on the cross for me and rose again, and I confess You as my Savior and Lord. Forgive me, and show me how to live for Your glory. Come into my life. Make me new. Help me walk in Your truth. Amen.*

If you prayed that prayer, heaven celebrates you (Luke 15:7), and you've begun the greatest journey of your life, a journey not defined by what you carry, but by Who carries you. You were made for *this*! This life lived in the fullness and freedom of Christ, the One who is your *More*.

→ *Next Step:* Turn to the Appendix in this book and read "What Do I Do Now? After Accepting Christ as Savior." It will guide you through your first steps as a new believer.

Naomi may have called herself *bitter*, but Ruth refused to let go. In that moment of choice, the story turned. When Orpah kissed Naomi goodbye and returned to Moab, Ruth clung tighter—not just to Naomi, but to Naomi's God. Her words became the hinge of redemption, the moment everything began to change:

If Naomi had truly been beyond hope, why would Ruth have followed her? Even in despair, Naomi's faith—though weary—was still a witness strong enough to draw Ruth away from Moab and into the story of redemption. Ruth left behind her culture, her idols, her family customs, and everything familiar to follow Naomi and her God. She didn't know what the future held, but her trust tied her to a destiny she could not yet see.

That single act of radical trust became the divine turning point— not only for Ruth and Naomi but for generations to come. The widow from Moab became part of the lineage of King David and, ultimately, of Jesus Christ Himself.

Naomi thought her name was *Mara*—bitter. But God was already rewriting her story through Ruth's faithfulness. Naomi's journey reminds us that grief and lies can rename us, weigh us down, and even make us question if God has abandoned us. Yet, in the hands of a faithful God, even emptiness becomes the soil where redemption takes root.

Faith That Follows

Standing beside Naomi was Ruth, a young woman from Moab who saw something in her mother-in-law's God that was worth leaving everything behind to follow. Both Ruth and Orpah were given the same invitation—to return to what was familiar or to follow Naomi into the unknown. Orpah chose comfort and certainty; Ruth chose covenant and faith.

That choice reveals something profound. Why would a Moabite woman—raised among idols and foreign gods—turn her back on everything she knew to follow

> *"In the hands of a Faithful God, even emptiness becomes the soil where redemption takes root."*

the God of Israel? It could only be because she saw the authenticity of Naomi's faith. Even in her grief and emptiness, Naomi must have reflected a quiet confidence that her God was still good. Naomi had no husband, no sons, no possessions—she was truly empty. And yet her steadfastness, even in loss, spoke louder than any sermon. Ruth believed because she saw a faith worth following.

Ruth clung to Naomi and chose to adopt her as more than a mother-in-law but as a mother. She told her I will go where you go, your people will be my people, and your God will be my God. With these words, she was stepping into a life of trust and surrender before knowing how the story would unfold. She had no guarantees, no promise of provision, no idea how they would eat, or where they would live. But she chose faith over familiarity, obedience over comfort, and love over fear.

That is what it looks like to walk in More. The More Life isn't found in knowing every detail; it's found in knowing the One who leads. Like Ruth, we are invited to cling to God even when the road ahead looks uncertain. Faith doesn't remove the emptiness; it transforms it. Ruth followed Naomi into Bethlehem with nothing in her hands but trust, and God filled her emptiness with redemption. Through her faithfulness came a lineage that led to David, and ultimately to Jesus, the Redeemer of us all.

When God calls you to leave the familiar—to step away from your own "Moab" of comfort, security, or fear—remember Ruth's story. What you leave behind cannot compare to what God is leading you toward. *Cling to Him.* He will turn your emptiness into abundance and your faithfulness into a legacy that outlives you.

Before Your Next Step
Before you step into what's next, pause and take this in: Freedom begins when you

> *"The More Life isn't found in knowing every detail; it's found in knowing the One who leads."*

---

stop agreeing with the lies that tried to define you. You are not what you've lost, what someone else said about you, or what you once believed about yourself. You are who God says you are—chosen, loved, and called.

Like Ruth, you may not know how the next chapter of your life will unfold. The path may feel uncertain, and what lies ahead may seem as empty as Naomi's hands when she returned to Bethlehem. But remember this: God does some of His most beautiful work in the places that feel barren. When you dare to trust Him, when you cling to His promises more tightly than your fears, He begins to rewrite your story with grace.

The same God who turned Naomi's bitterness into blessing and Ruth's faithfulness into legacy is the One who is writing your story even now. Every surrendered "yes" becomes a seed He plants for your future harvest. So, lift your eyes, beloved; your Redeemer lives, and He is not finished with you yet. Let this be your declaration as you step forward: *Lord, I believe Your truth more than my past. I will cling to You even when I don't see the way ahead.*

What you leave behind may feel uncertain, but what lies before you is overflowing with promise. The next chapter invites you to step boldly into that trust—to walk not by sight, but by faith— into the More Life you were made to live.

Selah: Lay Down the Lies

"Therefore, if any man be in Christ, he is a new creature: old things are passed away; behold, all things are become new" (2 Corinthians 5:17 KJV).

From the very beginning, God's question has echoed through time: *"Who told you that?"*

It was the question He asked Adam and Eve after they hid in shame, and it is the same question He still asks us today. It is not one of accusation but of awakening— a divine call for us to trace the source of every false word we've believed. *Who told you that you were unworthy? Who said you were too broken, too late, too small, or too much?*

The enemy's voice may be subtle, but truth speaks louder. God never named you unworthy. He never labeled you disqualified. He never called you less than. Those names never came from Him. When He looks at you, He calls you beloved, chosen, and free.

Imagine yourself standing before the Father, hands full of heavy suitcases labeled *fear, shame, comparison, perfectionism, performance, procrastination,* and *suppression.* These weights have shaped how you've seen yourself—but they were never meant to define you. One by one, lay them at His feet. Let Him replace the weight of those lies with the lightness of His truth. And as you lay them down, hear His invitation again: "Come unto me, all ye that labour and are heavy laden, and I will give you rest" (Matthew 11:28 KJV).

This is not just an invitation to peace— it's an invitation to a Person. The More Life you've been searching for is found in Jesus Himself. He came so that you could live fully, freely, and abundantly: "The thief cometh not, but for to steal, and to kill, and to destroy: I am come that they might have life, and that they might have it more abundantly" (John 10:10 KJV).

Like Ruth standing beside Naomi, you now stand at a crossroads. Ruth and Orpah both heard the same invitation—to return home or to follow forward. Orpah turned back to what was safe, but Ruth clung to what was true. She left behind everything familiar to follow the God she had come to believe was real.

Ruth's story reminds us that faith sometimes looks like walking away from the known with nothing but trust in your hands. She left her home, her idols, and her comfort behind, choosing instead to follow Naomi's God, even when she didn't know how they would survive. Yet that decision led her straight into God's redemptive plan.

In the same way, God is calling you to leave behind your own "Moab"—the places of comfort, fear, and false identity—and to step into His truth. Freedom begins when you stop agreeing with the lies that tried to define you and start clinging to the truth of who He says you are.

Take a deep breath. Let go. Rest in the truth that the same God who turned Naomi's emptiness into abundance and Ruth's faithfulness into legacy can do the same for you.

> *"Freedom begins when you stop agreeing with the lies that tried to define you and start clinging to the truth of who He says you are."*

Pause & Reflect

- Which lie or false label have I carried the longest?
- What "suitcase" am I still dragging that God has asked me to lay down?
- Where is God calling me to leave behind my "Moab"— my comfort zones, false names, or old patterns—and step into His truth?
- What does it mean for me to "cling to God" like Ruth did, even when the outcome is uncertain?
- How does knowing Christ personally invite me into the More Life He promised?

Write honestly. Pray deeply. Let His presence steady you as you reflect.

Prayer of Gratitude and Renewal
Father, thank You for asking the question that leads me back to truth.

I lay down every lie I've carried—every false name, every heavy burden.

I surrender the fear, shame, and striving that have kept me from freedom.

Replace them with the peace of knowing who I am in You.

Thank You for calling me beloved, chosen, and free.

Like Ruth, I choose to cling to You even when I don't see the way ahead.

Lead me from my "Moab" into the fullness of Your promise.

Let Your truth take root in my heart until Your voice becomes the only one I follow.

In Jesus' name, Amen.

Action Step: Replacing the Lie with Truth
Write down one lie or label that has held you back. Then, cross it out and write a truth from God's Word in its place. Speak that truth aloud every morning this week—let heaven hear you and let your heart believe it.

O — OVERCOME WHAT HOLDS YOU BACK

Breaking agreements with fear, lies, wounds, and
limiting narratives

*"For God did not give us a spirit of fear, but of power,
love and self-discipline."*
2 TIMOTHY 1:7 (NIV)

CHAPTER 3
The Question of Trust
Choosing Faith Over Fear

Jesus once asked His disciples in the middle of a storm: "Why are you so afraid? Do you still have no faith?" (Mark 4:40). It is the tender but piercing question He still asks us today: *Will you trust Me?*

Fear and trust cannot coexist. Fear paralyzes. Trust pulls you forward. Fear keeps you clinging to what you know. Trust invites you to step into the unknown. Again and again, God leads us into places where the question becomes unavoidable: *Do you trust Me here?*

In Chapter 2, we laid down the lies and labels that weighed us down. We unzipped every suitcase of fear, shame, perfectionism, and comparison, and set them at the feet of Jesus. We watched as Naomi and Ruth's story showed us that faith can rise even from the ashes of loss.

> *"Fear and trust cannot coexist. Fear paralyzes. Trust pulls you forward."*

Now, the journey continues. The next step toward living the More Life is *trust*.

Trust is what bridges the gap between where we've been and where God is leading. It's the quiet confidence that, even when we don't understand the "why," we can still rest in the "Who." Like Ruth following Naomi toward Bethlehem, we, too, are invited to follow God into places that feel uncertain but are pregnant with promise.

Brandon's Diagnosis: "Lord, I Trust You"

It was a summer afternoon in 2003 when I was driving home from the hospital, weary and hollow. My son Brandon had just undergone brain surgery, and though the doctors spoke in cautious terms, the uncertainty hung heavy in the air.

That year had already been marked by personal grief. In January, one of my beloved first-grade students, Brittany, passed away from multiple brain tumors. In March, a college friend and sister in Christ called me to pray for her son, explaining that the doctors had given up hope. Although we prayed that evening, he too passed away. And now, in June, I was sitting in the same waiting room in the same hospital, with some of the same neurologists and brain surgeons, hearing the same terrifying words as my college friend and the mother of my beloved student: *tumor*. The weight was crushing.

At home that afternoon, I dropped my bags on the floor and headed to the bathroom to prepare for spending another night at the hospital. But before I could turn on the water, I sank to my knees next to the tub, too broken for words. I wanted to pray for healing, but no words would come. My heart was too raw.

Finally, from the depths of my soul, four words broke through: "Lord, I trust You."

That was all I had. No eloquence. No certainty. Just surrender.

And in that moment, God's presence filled the room. Peace wrapped around me like a covering, even though the battle wasn't over. Brandon still faced weeks of vomiting, dizziness, setbacks, another surgery, and years of follow-ups. But I learned something that day: Trust is not about quick fixes or guaranteed outcomes. Trust is about presence—God Himself showing up, His nearness becoming the miracle.

The Stone Mountain Climb: Persevering One Step at a Time

Stone Mountain rises out of the Georgia landscape like a giant, gray challenge. From the bottom, the summit looks impossibly high. I remember the day I joined a group to climb it. At first, excitement carried me along. But halfway up, my legs burned, my lungs ached, and the sun beat down mercilessly. The top still seemed impossibly far. Fear whispered, "You'll never make it. Stop here."

> *"Trust is not about having all the answers—it's about leaning the full weight of your heart on the One who does."*

But around me, others pressed on. Some moved quickly, some paused to catch their breath, and no one mocked the ones who had slowed down. That gave me the strength to keep going. One small step. Then another. And another. When I finally reached the summit, the exhaustion was real, but so was the joy. The mountain hadn't moved. But I had.

That climb taught me something: Trust is not about sprinting up the mountain. It's about persevering in small steps, even when fear tells you to quit.

And that's really the essence of trust. It's not about having all the answers or knowing how everything will turn out. Proverbs 3:5–6 says, "Trust in the LORD with all your heart, and lean not on your own understanding; in all your ways submit to him, and he will make your paths straight."

Trust asks us to lean the full weight of our hearts on God, not on our own reasoning, not on our own control, not on the fear of what might be. Fear wants to paralyze us. Trust moves us forward. Fear depends on what we can see. Trust depends on Who we know.

Every act of trust is really a surrendered yes: *Yes, Lord, I'll lean on You. Yes, Lord, I'll take the next step even when the path isn't clear. Yes, Lord, I'll follow Your leading instead of my own logic.*

Biblical Examples of Trust
That's what Peter, Esther, Deborah, and Abigail all discovered when they decided to put their trust in the Lord. Each faced a moment or moments that demanded courage beyond human strength, storms that tested their obedience and faith. For Peter, it was a storm at sea. For Esther, a throne room filled with danger. For Deborah, a battlefield where faith became leadership. And for Abigail, a moment of divine discernment that saved her household.

Every one of them reached a turning point when fear could have paralyzed them, but trust pulled them forward. Their stories remind us that trust isn't the absence of fear. It's the decision to keep walking toward God, even when fear is shouting louder than faith.

Peter: Fear Paralyzes, Trust Pulls Forward (Matthew 14:22–31)
The storm raged across the Sea of Galilee. The disciples strained at the oars, wind whipping against their faces, hearts pounding with exhaustion and fear. Then, through the chaos, they saw a figure walking toward them on the waves. Panic seized them. "It's a ghost!" they cried out in terror (verse 26). But then came a voice they knew. It was Jesus, the calm within the storm: "Take courage! It is I. Don't be afraid" (verse 27).

Peter's heart raced. The same sea that terrified him was now the place where his faith would be tested. "Lord, if it's You," he said, "tell me to come to You on the water" (verse 28). And Jesus simply answered, "Come."

In that instant, Peter had a choice: to stay in the safety of the boat or to step out into the impossible. The boat represented logic, comfort, and control. The water represented faith, risk, and dependence. Eleven disciples stayed seated, clinging to what felt secure, but one—just one—had the courage to move.

Gripping the edge of the boat, Peter lifted one trembling foot over the side and stepped forward. For a moment, he did the impossible. The waves beneath him held. His eyes locked on Jesus, and fear was silenced by faith. But then the wind howled louder, the waves rose higher, and Peter's focus shifted. He looked at the storm instead of the Savior and he began to sink. "Lord, save me!" he cried (verse 30). Immediately, Jesus reached out His hand and caught him. "You of little faith," He said, "why did you doubt?" (verse 31).

Peter's story reminds us that trust doesn't always mean walking perfectly. It means stepping out when others stay seated. It means choosing obedience even when fear screams louder than faith. Trust requires the courage to move when the outcome is uncertain, believing that even if you sink, Jesus will catch you.

The same waters that threatened to drown Peter became the very place where he experienced God's power. When Jesus lifted him back up, He wasn't just rescuing Peter from the storm; He was revealing what's possible when we fix our eyes on Him instead of our circumstances.

Trust pulls us forward—out of the boat of fear, out of the safety of control, and into the wild, miraculous places where God meets us. Like Peter, every step of faith we take toward Jesus, no matter how small, is a declaration that says, "Lord, I trust You more than what I see."

Esther: If I Perish, I Perish (Esther 4:12–16)

Esther lived in a palace of risk. When her people faced extermination, she alone had access to the king. Yet she knew the law: To approach without invitation meant death, just as Queen Vashti had been banished before her.

Fear said, "Stay silent. Protect yourself." But trust spoke louder. Esther called her people to fast, and then declared, "I will go to the king, even though it is against the law. And if I perish, I perish" (verse 16).

She didn't know the outcome. She risked everything. And her trust became the hinge of deliverance for her people. It's what Esther embodied when she declared, "If I perish, I perish," risking her life to stand before the king.

Deborah: Trusting God's Word Above Culture (Judges 4–5)

For twenty years, Israel lived under Canaanite oppression. But Deborah, a prophetess and judge, trusted God's word. She called Barak to lead Israel's army, declaring God's promise of victory. Barak wavered: "If you go with me, I will go; but if you don't go with me, I won't go" (Judges 4:8).

Deborah stood firm. She trusted God's authority above culture's expectations. She went, and the Lord gave victory, proving His word true. Deborah displayed a surrendered "yes" when she rose to lead Israel into battle, even when the men hesitated.

Trust is standing on God's promise, even when others hesitate.

Abigail: Wisdom in the Face of Danger (1 Samuel 25)

When Nabal insulted David, wrath boiled inside David. He strapped on his sword and set out to destroy Nabal's household. But Abigail moved quickly. She rode out to meet David with food, wisdom, and humility.

Facing an angry warrior, she spoke words that turned wrath into restraint: "The LORD your God will certainly make a lasting dynasty for my lord, because you fight the LORD's battles. Let no wrongdoing be found in you as long as you live" (verse 28).

Her trust in God's wisdom saved her household and kept David from bloodshed. Sometimes trust looks like courage wrapped in discernment.

Courage takes many forms: leadership, sacrifice, loyalty, and wisdom. Each of these individuals leaned not on their own understanding but on God's leading. Their yes became the doorway into God's More.

Trust is always the doorway into More. Each story we've encountered reveals what happens when faith moves beyond comfort and into obedience.

Peter's trust pulled him out of the boat when others stayed seated. Esther's trust gave her courage to speak when silence seemed safer. Deborah's trust brought victory to a nation. Abigail's trust in God's wisdom preserved her household from destruction.

Each story reminds us that trust is not passive! It's active faith in motion. It's what bridges the gap between where you are and the More Life God has waiting for you.

The More Life is not reserved for the fearless but for those who choose to believe God's promises more than their fears. It's for

---

those who dare to step forward, speak up, and surrender even when the outcome is uncertain. Trust is the bridge between the "what is" and the "what will be," between the storm and the shore, between surrender and supernatural peace.

Ephesians 3:20 says: "Now to Him who is able to do immeasurably more than all we ask or imagine, according to His power that is at work within us." Trust is the bridge to that life—one built not on certainty, but on confidence in the One who is faithful. Every act of trust opens the door for God to heal what fear once held captive.

Trust steadies our hearts so His restoring work can begin. It is the soil where faith takes root and wholeness starts to grow. When we stop striving to fix ourselves and start trusting the One who can, He turns broken places into testimonies of grace.

The next step on this journey is not just about believing; it's about becoming. Wholeness is God's answer to every fractured place within you. And as you'll soon discover, the same Savior who called Peter to walk on water is still asking a question that changes everything: *"Do you want to be made whole?"*

Selah: Trust Without Borders

"Trust in the LORD with all your heart and lean not on your own understanding; in all your ways submit to Him, and He will make your paths straight" (Proverbs 3:5–6).

Every storm, every waiting season, and every uncertain step carries the same quiet question from Jesus: "Why are you so afraid? Do you still have no faith?" (Mark 4:40).

You've seen it in Ruth, who followed God into the unknown.

You've seen it in Peter, who stepped out of the boat when others stayed seated.

You've seen it in Esther, who risked her life to stand for her people.

Each example shows us that trust is not a single moment. It's a posture of the heart. It's faith that moves forward, even when the outcome is uncertain. Trust does not silence fear by force; it transforms it through surrender. It isn't the absence of trembling. It's choosing to take the next step even while your knees shake. Trust doesn't demand understanding; it invites alignment. It doesn't guarantee outcomes; it guarantees His presence.

When Peter stepped out of the boat, the storm didn't stop. But he walked anyway. When Esther stood before the king, she didn't know the ending. But she obeyed anyway. When Ruth left Moab, she couldn't see her future. But she followed anyway. And when you whisper, "Lord, I trust You," heaven hears faith louder than fear.

Take a deep breath. Picture the waters in your own life: the places that feel too deep, too uncertain, too impossible. Those are the very places where trust is born. God never asked you to calm the storm; He asked you to keep your eyes on Him through it.

Trust doesn't happen by accident; it grows in the soil of alignment. When your heart delights in the Lord, your plans yield to His will, and your steps follow His leading. Psalm 37:4–5 (NKJV) says: "Delight yourself also in the LORD, and He shall give you the desires of your heart. Commit your way to the LORD, trust also in Him, and He shall bring it to pass." Here's a battle plan for trust, based on God's Word:

1. *Pray before you step.* Anchor every action in prayer.
2. *Name your fear.* Speak it so truth can silence it.
3. *Take one small step.* Trust grows in motion.
4. *Surround yourself with encouragers.* Courage is contagious.
5. *Celebrate small victories.* Remember His faithfulness.

Pause & Reflect

- Where is God asking me to step out of the boat and trust Him?

> *"Courage is contagious."*

- What fear is keeping me anchored when He's calling me to move?
- When have I seen God's presence become the miracle before the outcome changed?

Write honestly. Pray deeply. Let His presence steady you as you reflect.

Prayer of Trust and Alignment

Father, I choose to trust You with my whole heart.

I surrender my fears, my plans, and my need to understand.

Teach me to acknowledge You in every step: big or small.

Align my desires with Yours and direct my path toward Your perfect will.

Strengthen my heart until trust pulls me forward where fear once held me back.

You are my courage, my peace, my steady hand on the water.

I trust You beyond my feelings, beyond my sight, beyond my understanding.

In Jesus' name, Amen.

Action Step: A Visible Declaration of Faith

Write down the greatest fear or uncertainty you're facing. Underneath it, declare in bold: **Even if; I trust God.** Place it where you'll see it often, as a daily reminder that trust is stronger than fear and that God's presence goes before you in every step.

CHAPTER 4
"Do You Want to Be Made Whole?"
Healing & Transformation

"Do you want to be made whole?" (John 5:6 KJV). It's a piercing question Jesus asked a man who had been lying by a pool for thirty-eight years, waiting to be healed. It's also the same question He asks us today.

Most of us carry an ache for wholeness. We long for healing in our bodies, peace in our minds, and restoration in our hearts. We want broken relationships mended, old wounds healed, and lost joy found again. Yet so often, we live right on the edge of transformation, wishing, waiting, longing, but never moving.

To be made *whole* is not simply to be fixed; it is to be restored to God's original

> *"Do you want to be made whole?"*

design, which is His divine purpose and intent for our lives. Wholeness is the process of becoming who God created you to be before pain, fear, or disappointment tried to rewrite your story. It's not perfection, it's alignment. It's when every fragmented part of your life—mind, body, spirit, and soul—is gathered and redeemed by the One who made you.

The Hebrew word that captures this beautifully is *shalom*. Often translated as "peace," it actually means far more. *Shalom* speaks of

---

wholeness, completeness, soundness, safety, and harmony. When Scripture repeats it—*shalom, shalom*—it's emphasizing a peace that is layered and lasting. Isaiah 26:3 says, "You will keep in perfect peace (*shalom, shalom*) those whose minds are steadfast, because they trust in You." It's not the absence of trouble, but the presence of divine order and restoration.

Wholeness, then, is to walk in *shalom, shalom*—a peace that heals the heart, aligns the soul, and restores us to God's intended rhythm of life.

The Bible gives us two powerful portraits of healing: a woman who pressed through a crowd in faith, and a man who remained on his mat, rehearsing excuses. Both encountered Jesus. Both had the opportunity to be made whole. Their stories still speak to us today, calling us out of shame, fear, and passivity into the healing and transformation only Christ can bring.

> "Wholeness begins when we stop surviving and start surrendering."

The Woman with the Issue of Blood (Mark 5:25–34)
She had carried her secret pain for twelve long years. Every sunrise reminded her of her weakness; every sunset marked another day of isolation. Her body betrayed her—bleeding without ceasing—and society branded her unclean. She couldn't worship in the temple. She couldn't freely embrace her family. Whispers followed her in the marketplace. Her name had been overshadowed by her condition: *the bleeding woman.*

She had tried everything. Doctors made confident promises but left her pockets empty and her heart heavy. Remedies that once sparked hope only deepened her despair when they failed. Her strength dwindled. Her resources vanished. But even when her hope grew thin, her ache for healing never disappeared.

Then one morning, word spread through her village: *Jesus is here.*

She had heard the stories: blind eyes opening, the lame walking, the tormented set free. Something stirred within her that had been dormant for years: *faith*. Desperation met determination. She told herself, *If I can just touch the hem of His garment, I will be healed.*

The streets were crowded. People pressed in from every direction. Shame whispered, "You don't belong here." Fear shouted, "What if He rejects you? What if they recognize you?" But faith spoke louder. And so with trembling hands, she pushed through the crowd, refusing to be denied.

Finally, she saw Him. Crouching low, she reached out, her fingers brushing the fringe of His robe.

Instantly—not gradually, not eventually, *instantly*—the bleeding stopped. Healing rushed through her like light flooding darkness. She felt strength returning to her body and peace settling over her spirit.

And then Jesus stopped. He turned and asked, "Who touched Me?" The disciples laughed. *Everyone is touching you!* But Jesus knew. Power had gone out from Him.

The woman froze. She had wanted to be healed in secret, to slip away unnoticed. Instead, she found herself face-to-face with the One who saw everything. Trembling, she fell before Him and confessed the whole truth.

Jesus didn't shame her. He called her *daughter*. Not outcast. Not unclean. *Daughter.* Then he said words that reached deeper than her physical body: "And he said unto her, Daughter, thy faith hath made thee whole; go in peace, and be whole of thy plague" (Mark 5:34 KJV).

He didn't just heal her body; He restored her identity. In that moment, she stepped into *shalom, shalom*—perfect peace and complete restoration.

This woman's story is more than history; it's a mirror. Healing often requires pressing past shame and fear. Her courage asks us to pause and consider: *What crowd do I need to press through in order to reach my healing?*

Maybe it's the crowd of opinions—the fear of what others will think if you step forward. Maybe it's the crowd of memories—old wounds replaying their pain like a familiar song. Or maybe it's the crowd of excuses—the quiet belief that healing is for everyone else but you.

> "He didn't just heal her body; He restored her identity."

The woman in Mark 5 didn't let her label define her. For twelve years, the world called her *unclean*, but Jesus called her *daughter*. Her faith didn't begin in a place of strength; it began in weakness, in weariness, in the decision to reach out to Jesus anyway. That's the place where transformation begins—when we reach for Jesus instead of rehearsing rejection.

Faith doesn't wait for us to feel worthy—it moves in spite of the unworthy feelings. The woman's healing began the moment she reached beyond what she could see. Wholeness begins the same way for us—it begins when faith becomes louder than fear. When we stop hiding behind shame and start pressing toward the Savior, the power that once passed through the streets begins to move through us. When we reach for Him, He reaches back. The touch that healed the woman's body is the same touch that still restores hearts today.

The Man at the Pool of Bethesda (John 5:1–9)

The pool was crowded that day, as it often was. Bethesda: "House of Mercy." Five shaded porches lined with mats and makeshift beds, filled with people who were blind, lame, and paralyzed. They came with hope but often left with disappointment in their hearts.

An angel was said to stir the waters occasionally, and whoever stepped in first was healed. But for most, the water became a cruel

> "Wholeness begins the same way for us—it begins when faith becomes louder than fear."

reminder that healing was always just out of reach. Among the people lay a man who had been sick for thirty-eight years—a man who had spent almost four decades watching others move ahead while he stayed behind. His life was confined to a mat, defined by what he couldn't do, what he'd lost, and what no one else had done for him.

Then Jesus entered Bethesda. He didn't go to the fastest or the strongest; He went straight to the man who had been lying there the longest. Kneeling beside him, Jesus looked into his eyes and asked the question that pierced through years of pain: "Wilt thou be made whole?" (verse 6 KJV).

It almost sounds cruel, but it wasn't. Jesus wasn't questioning his desire; He was awakening it.

The man didn't answer with faith; he answered with excuses: "Sir, I have no man, when the water is troubled, to put me into the pool: but while I am coming, another steppeth down before me" (verse 7 KJV). In other words: *It's not my fault. I've been overlooked. I can't.*

But Jesus wasn't bound by superstition or the limits of the man's help. He looked beyond excuses and spoke a word that redefined the man's reality: "Rise, take up thy bed, and walk" (verse 8 KJV). Immediately, strength surged through the man's legs. Muscles that had been dormant for decades leapt to life. He stood. For the first time in thirty-eight years, he walked and carried the very mat that had once carried him.

Excuses keep us stuck in the same place. We can spend years lying on the mat of our pain, blaming others, waiting for the "perfect moment." But healing begins when we respond in faith to the voice of Jesus, even when it doesn't make sense.

What excuses have you been rehearsing instead of saying yes to Jesus' invitation to be made whole? What "mat" are you still lying on that He is calling you to pick up? Sometimes, the miracle happens the moment we stop rehearsing our reasons and start rising in obedience.

The Call to Rise

There comes a point when waiting for someone else to rescue you is no longer an option. I've lived there, praying prayers that sounded holy but were rooted in hopelessness, asking God to change my circumstances while I refused to take the step of faith He was calling me to.

The man at the pool did it for thirty-eight years. The woman with the issue of blood lost twelve years to it. And yet, in His mercy, Jesus didn't let them stay there. He came to them and asked the same question He still asks us today: "Do you want to be made whole?"

He wasn't being cruel. He was revealing the heart posture. *Are you willing to let go of your excuses, your fears, and your patterns of self-pity?*

Self-pity may feel comforting, but it's a silent thief of destiny. Disappointment can drain our hope until survival feels safer than transformation. Maybe you've believed before, and it didn't turn out the way you'd hoped. Maybe you've prayed, and the answer seemed delayed. But God is still asking: *Will you believe again? Will you press into My presence again? Will you let Me do what only I can do?*

Passivity is not faith; it's surrender to the wrong thing. God's plan isn't for us to stay paralyzed by life, waiting for others to move us. His plan is for us to respond when He speaks, to rise when He calls, and to move forward even when our legs still tremble.

A Word About Wholeness and Healing

When Jesus asked, "Do you want to be made whole?" His question was never limited to physical restoration; it was always about the total transformation of the soul.

This is not an indictment of anyone who lives with chronic physical or mental conditions. I have personally known and deeply admired believers who walk through daily challenges with profound faith, peace, and purpose. Their lives are radiant testimonies of what true wholeness looks like in Christ. That's because wholeness is not the absence of struggle; it is the presence of peace in the midst of it. Katie Mathews, who wrote the powerful book *Unparalyzed* and is someone I know personally through my coach training work with Dream Releaser Coaching, has so encouraged me with her faith and joy. Katherine Wolf, the author of *Suffer Strong: How to Survive Anything by Redefining Everything*, reminds us that we can be limited in body yet fully alive in purpose. Both Katie and Katherine embody the truth that our brokenness does not disqualify us from God's power. In fact, it often becomes the very platform for His glory.

The focus of this chapter is not merely on physical healing, but on *spiritual transformation for ministry*, learning to rise above excuses, fears, and limitations so that Christ's strength is revealed through our surrender.

When we walk in spiritual wholeness, even in weakness, we live out the More Life that Christ promised—a life where His strength is made perfect in our surrender, and His grace is sufficient in every place we feel limited.

Layers of Healing
Wholeness rarely happens all at once. God often heals in layers—like the gentle peeling back of bandages from an old wound, exposing what needs to breathe in the light of His love. Sometimes healing begins in the body; other times, it begins in the heart. But make no mistake—every layer matters.

When Jesus asked the man at the pool of Bethesda, "Do you want to be made whole?" (John 5:6), He wasn't just asking about physical recovery. He was inviting the man into total restoration: body, mind, and soul. To be "made whole" means to live in alignment with the way God originally designed us: healed, free, at peace, and in right relationship with Him and others.

Wholeness is more than recovery; it is renewal. It is the moment when what once broke you becomes a testimony of His power.

Sometimes God heals the surface first: the visible wounds, the addictions, the illnesses that draw our immediate attention. But often, His deeper work begins beneath the surface. He gently touches the unseen fractures: the bitterness we've nursed in silence, the unforgiveness we've justified, the lies we've believed about our worth. He unravels fear thread by thread until we can breathe freely again.

Healing in layers means we learn to trust Him one surrender at a time. It's the process of giving Him access to the locked rooms of our hearts, the ones marked *Do Not Enter*. Maybe you've let Him touch your circumstances, but He's asking to touch your identity. Maybe He's healed a relationship, but now He's after your mindset. Maybe He's restored your energy, but now He wants to restore your joy. Each layer reveals another opportunity to respond to His question: "Do you want to be made whole?"

And when we say yes, God begins His sacred work of reordering the soul. He replaces despair with hope, fear with faith, and shame with belonging. He restores the sound of laughter that sorrow once silenced. He makes peace where there was chaos, clarity where there was confusion, and purpose where there was pain.

This is the miracle of wholeness. It's not only about what you're healed *from*, but what you're healed *for*. Wholeness positions you to walk in purpose. It allows you to love without guarding your heart, to give without fear of lack, and to believe again after disappointment.

You may not see every layer of healing all at once, but rest assured: God wastes nothing. Each season of surrender draws you closer to His image, closer to the person you were always meant to be. Healing is not a single event; it's a lifelong invitation into the wholeness of Christ.

So, if you're still waiting for the final piece to fall into place, don't lose heart. The same Jesus who asked, "Do you want to be made whole?" is still standing beside you, ready to finish what He began. The layers may take time, but His touch is making all things new; one healing at a time.

Living the *More* Life

Living the More Life means refusing to settle for the status quo. It's not just about being healed; it's about being *made whole*: spiritually aligned, emotionally free, and ready to fulfill your purpose.

Healing is never meant to end at comfort; it's meant to lead to *calling*. When Jesus restores us, He doesn't just put us back together so we can return to life as usual. He restores us so we can rise, walk, and *serve*.

The woman who touched the hem of Jesus' garment didn't fade into the crowd; she walked away with a testimony that changed her community. The man who once lay by the pool didn't just stand; he carried his mat through the city as a living witness that mercy moves mountains.

Wholeness is not only God's gift to you; it's His investment in you. Every healed place becomes a testimony, and every testimony becomes a tool God can use to reach others. When you are made whole, you don't just *survive* the storm; you come out carrying something.

Battle Plan for Healing & Transformation

Healing and transformation are not passive experiences—they are sacred partnerships. God does the restoring, but we participate in the renewal. Just as the woman with the issue of blood *pressed through* to touch Jesus, and the man at Bethesda *got up* when Jesus called his name, transformation requires response. Healing begins the moment we engage our faith in action.

Here's your Battle Plan for Healing & Transformation. It is a spiritual blueprint for walking in wholeness, one step at a time.

1. Acknowledge Your Ache

Before healing begins, you must name the ache. God cannot heal what we continue to hide. Be honest about where you're hurting, what feels broken, or what still bleeds beneath the surface. Say it out loud. Write it in your journal. Bring it into the light of His presence.

Jesus asked the man by the pool, "Do you want to be made whole?" He asked this not because He didn't know the answer, but because the man needed to acknowledge his own longing. Awareness opens the door to restoration.

"The Lord is close to the brokenhearted and saves those who are crushed in spirit" (Psalm 34:18).

2. Press Through the Crowd

Shame will whisper, "You don't belong here." Fear will tell you, "It's too late." But faith says, "Keep moving." Like the woman who reached for Jesus' garment, you must press through the opinions, the doubts, and the distractions that crowd your mind.

Wholeness requires persistence. The crowd might be your past, your self-doubt, or the memories that haunt you. Whatever it is, don't stop pressing. Healing is found in the reach.

"Let us run with perseverance the race marked out for us, fixing our eyes on Jesus" (Hebrews 12:1–2).

3. Respond to His Voice

When Jesus speaks, movement is required. His words carry power, but they also demand participation. When He says, "Get up," don't delay. Rise, even if your legs still tremble. Step, even if your faith feels small. The man at Bethesda could have stayed on his mat, but obedience turned his waiting place into a walking place.

Every healing begins with a response. Transformation happens when our faith translates into motion.

"My sheep listen to My voice; I know them, and they follow Me" (John 10:27).

4. Walk in Your Healing
Healing is both a moment and a movement. The moment is when Jesus touches you, and the movement is what you do afterward. The woman healed of her issue of blood didn't just return home quietly; she left forever changed, walking in her new identity as *daughter*.

To walk in your healing means to live like you are free. Stop rehearsing the pain and start declaring the promise. Walk with the confidence that what Jesus has done in you is real, lasting, and meant to be seen.

"For we live by faith, not by sight" (2 Corinthians 5:7).

5. Guard Your Wholeness
Every miracle needs maintenance. Wholeness is not self-sustaining—it's sustained through intimacy with God.

Stay connected to the Healer through prayer, worship, and gratitude. Guard your heart from bitterness, unbelief, or distractions that try to reopen what God has closed. Healing is not a moment to visit—it's a lifestyle to protect.

"Above all else, guard your heart, for everything you do flows from it" (Proverbs 4:23).

6. Use What's Been Healed
Every scar has a story, and every healed place carries purpose. Don't hide what God has restored—use it. Ask Him how He wants to

use your renewed strength, your restored faith, and your redeemed story to help others find healing too. The woman who touched Jesus didn't just receive healing; she became a testimony. You are not healed to be silent; you are healed to be sent. Healing is never the end; it's the beginning of a new assignment.

Wholeness always leads to purpose. When you rise from the place of healing, God places something in your hand. It is something that carries the power to bless, to serve, and to build His Kingdom. The woman who touched the hem of Jesus' garment didn't just walk away healed; she walked away *whole*. Her story became a living testimony that pointed others to the Healer. The same is true for you. Every scar tells a story. Every layer of restoration carries a divine purpose.

The question is no longer, "Do you want to be made whole?" Now, the question becomes, "What will you do with what I've given you?"

Healing was God's invitation to transformation; purpose is His call to participation. You've been restored so that others might find restoration through you. The places where you were once broken are now places of divine strength, evidence that God still makes all things new.

Healing was never meant to stop at you. It was meant to flow *through* you. That's where we'll turn next, discovering how your healing, your gifts, and your story can become instruments of God's *More* in the world.

Selah: Rise and Walk
"Jesus said to him, 'Rise, take up thy bed, and walk'" (John 5:8 KJV).

There comes a moment when waiting must give way to willingness. It happens when Jesus looks at you, not to expose your pain but to awaken your faith, and asks again: "Do you want to be made whole?"

Wholeness begins with honesty. It asks you to confront the excuses that have felt like protection, to release the fears that have become too familiar. It's not about striving for perfection; it's about surrendering to His presence.

The woman with the issue of blood pressed through the crowd, and the man at the pool obeyed a word that seemed impossible. Both discovered that healing doesn't begin when circumstances change; it begins when we move at His word.

Take a moment to breathe deeply. See yourself in the story: the crowd pressing close, the Savior turning toward you. Hear His voice cutting through the noise of your excuses, your fears, your disappointments: "Get up! Pick up your mat and walk."

Pause & Reflect
- Where do I most long for wholeness—physical, emotional, relational, or spiritual?
- What excuses or fears have kept me lying in the same place for too long?
- What crowd or label have I allowed to stand between me and my healing?
- What step of faith is Jesus calling me to take today?

Write honestly. Pray deeply. Let His presence steady you as you reflect.

My Declaration of Faith
Today, I choose to rise. I will take up my mat and walk.

Prayer of Healing and Trust

Lord, I hear Your question: Do you want to be made whole?

My answer is yes.

I surrender every excuse, every fear, every wound that has kept me bound.

I press through the crowd of shame and touch the hem of Your grace.

Speak Your word over me, and I will rise.

Let wholeness begin today—in my heart, my mind, my body, and my faith.

Amen.

Action Step

Write the phrase "I want to be made whole" on a piece of paper. Place it where you'll see it each morning. Say it aloud as a declaration of faith. Let it remind you: *Healing begins when you rise.*

R — RADIATE GOD'S PURPOSE & IMAGE

Shining boldly as the woman God designed you to be

"Let your light shine before others, that they may see your good deeds and glorify your Father in heaven."
MATTHEW 5:16 (NIV)

CHAPTER 5

"What Is in Your Hand?"
Restored to Reflect God's Purpose

Then the Lord said to him, "What is that in your hand?"
(Exodus 4:2)

M oses stood barefoot on holy ground, trembling before the burning bush. The air was heavy with the weight of destiny. The voice of God called him to confront Pharaoh and deliver a nation, yet Moses could only focus on what he lacked. He looked at his weathered staff and stammered: "What if they do not believe me or listen to me?"

Then the Lord said to him, "What is that in your hand?" (Exodus 4:2).

It wasn't much. Just a shepherd's stick: common, unimpressive, unremarkable. But once Moses surrendered that stick to God, it became an instrument of miracles. That same staff would one day stretch over the Red Sea, strike water from a rock, and become a symbol of God's authority and presence.

God doesn't use what you don't have. He uses what's already in your hand when you give it back to Him.

When You Feel Unqualified

We've all stood where Moses stood, staring at what God has placed before us and feeling painfully aware of what we lack.

Maybe it's not a staff, but a pen that's been gathering dust.

Maybe it's a business plan that feels too small to matter.

Maybe it's a story you've lived but haven't yet dared to tell.

Like Moses, we often respond to God's call with a list of limitations:

"But I'm not ready."

"But I don't have the resources."

"But what if they don't believe me?"

Yet the miracle doesn't start when we feel qualified; it begins when we surrender what's already in our hands.

> *"God never asks for what you don't have. He multiplies what you do."*

Because the same God who spoke from the bush still whispers to trembling hearts today, "I will be with you."

When Obedience Feels Small

We often expect our "yes" to God to look grand: visible, immediate, applauded. But most obedience begins in the quiet corners of life.

For Moses, it was a staff in the desert.

For the widow, it was a jar of oil in the kitchen.

For Peter, it was a net on the shore.

God trains us in the ordinary, so we'll be ready for the extraordinary. Each small act of faith: forgiving someone, showing up again, creating when no one is clapping, becomes the foundation of a greater calling. Don't underestimate the miracle in motion when you choose to obey God in the small things. Heaven keeps a record of faithfulness, not a list of followers.

Faithful Over Little, Ruler Over Much

It's easy to look around and wish we had someone else's platform, opportunity, or influence. But God doesn't measure greatness the way we do. He isn't asking for what's in someone else's hand; He's asking for what's in yours.

Maybe it's a voice, a skill, a compassion, a spreadsheet, or a small business idea. It might look ordinary, but in the hands of an extraordinary God, it becomes supernatural. And that's where stewardship begins, w hen what's been placed in your hand becomes what you faithfully offer back to Him. Jesus said it this way: "You have been faithful with a few things; I will put you in charge of many things" (Matthew 25:23).

Faithfulness is heaven's measure of readiness. The More Life that God calls you to isn't about doing more. It's about *becoming* more. It's about recognizing that what He's entrusted to you: your story, your talents, your influence, was never meant to stay buried or unused. God multiplies what you surrender.

Every gift carries Kingdom potential when it's yielded to the Giver. When you place the ordinary in His hands, He breathes on it until it becomes extraordinary. What once felt like simple obedience becomes supernatural impact. This is the next part of the journey: discovering what's in your hand and seeing how God wants to use it to reflect His image, reveal His goodness, and release His glory in the earth.

We often want the "many" before we've honored the "few." But the More Life is not built on ambition; it's built on stewardship. When you pause to thank God for what's already there, whether it's your family, your gifts, your story, or your opportunities, He multiplies it. But when you "despise" it or overlook it, even His blessings begin to feel like burdens.

Gratitude: The Posture of Multiplication
Gratitude changes the atmosphere of your heart. It's the posture that invites heaven to breathe on what seems small.

When Jesus broke bread and gave thanks, the loaves multiplied (see Matthew 14:19). When Paul and Silas sang hymns from a jail cell, chains fell off and doors flew open (see Acts 16:25–26). Gratitude opens doors that complaining keeps shut.

A grateful heart says, "God, You are enough. I trust Your timing." An entitled heart says, "I deserve more, and I deserve it now." Entitlement blinds you to grace. Gratitude magnifies it. It transforms the "not enough" into "more than enough."

When you learn to see what's in your hand as a gift from God, gratitude becomes the guardrail that keeps your heart in alignment. Purpose without gratitude quickly turns into striving, but gratitude keeps your purpose pure. First Thessalonians 5:16–18 says, "Rejoice always, pray continually, give thanks in all circumstances; for this is God's will for you in Christ Jesus." When you cultivate gratitude, you stop chasing More and start stewarding it.

Gratitude transforms the way you see your More. It shifts your focus from what's missing to what's been entrusted. When you cultivate gratitude, you stop chasing More and start *stewarding* it. Thanksgiving becomes the rhythm that sustains purpose . It is an anchor that keeps your soul steady when seasons change.

A grateful heart recognizes that every opportunity, every open door, and even every delay is part of God's divine design. Gratitude turns ordinary moments into sacred ground and reminds you that More is not about accumulation; it's about appreciation. It's not about having everything; it's about honoring the One who gave everything.

The Comparison Trap

If you constantly compare what's in your hand to what's in someone else's, you'll never see the miracle God is forming in yours. Comparison is a thief. It steals your peace and drains your joy. It tells you that you're behind when God says you're right on time. It whispers that your gift doesn't matter when heaven calls it essential. Envy is gratitude turned sour. Covetousness is believing the lie that God has a limited supply of blessings. But His Kingdom doesn't operate in scarcity. There's plenty of room for your calling, your creativity, and your contribution.

When you compare, you cancel your confidence. When you covet, you cripple your creativity. But when you're grateful, you become unstoppable because gratitude puts you in rhythm with grace.

Gratitude naturally leads to peace. When your heart is full of thanksgiving, it leaves little room for comparison. But when gratitude fades, envy quietly slips in, whispering that what God gave isn't enough. Scripture gives us this gentle reminder: "A heart at peace gives life to the body, but envy rots the bones" (Proverbs 14:30).

The *More Life* doesn't grow out of competition; it flourishes through contentment. You can't move forward while your eyes are fixed sideways. True peace begins when you stop measuring your progress against someone else's and start trusting God's timing for your own.

Contentment doesn't mean settling. It means resting in the rhythm of God's plan. It's knowing that what's in your hand is enough for the season you're in, and what's ahead will come when you're ready. Envy drains joy; peace restores it. When you choose contentment, you make room for creativity, clarity, and confidence to bloom again. The More Life is not about chasing someone else's calling. It's about flourishing in your own.

Don't Despise Small Beginnings

"Do not despise these small beginnings, for the Lord rejoices to see the work begin" (Zechariah 4:10 NLT). Most modern believers secretly overlook this verse because, if we're honest, we don't want the small beginnings. We want the big, bold, and instant success. But God doesn't rush growth. He roots it.

When my husband, Don, and I began ministry, we prayed a dangerous prayer: "Lord, don't let us take the elevator and skip steps. Let us take the steps, every single one, so we don't rise too fast and miss the character lessons we'll need to stay there."

The Enemy loves to push people to prominence before they have the maturity to sustain it. He wants us to sprint to the spotlight without the strength of humility or the discipline of dependence. But God builds differently. He trains us in the small, hidden places so our foundation can carry the weight of our future calling. Those early steps teach us endurance, patience, and faith. They teach us to serve unseen, to obey when no one's clapping, and to stay when it's hard. They teach us to value the process, not just the platform. That's why Scripture reminds us: "The steps of a good man are ordered by the LORD" (Psalm 37:23 KJV). It's not the elevator that prepares you; it's the steps. Don't despise the process that's shaping your promise.

Each step is intentional. God doesn't waste a single delay or detour; every season serves His design. The stairs you climb in secret are preparing you for the stages you'll one day stand on in public. Growth that's built step by step may feel slower, but it's stronger. The elevator can take you up fast, but only the steps teach you how to stand.

So don't despise the process that's shaping your promise. The same God who orders your steps is the One strengthening your stride. What feels hidden now is holy ground: the training place for the next level of your calling.

Blessing and Obedience Go Hand in Hand
In her book *Believe Bigger*, author Marshawn Evans Daniels writes, "God doesn't promise to bless us where we don't belong. But the blessing of His provision and protection is guaranteed to be upon His direction."

Blessing and obedience go hand in hand. We can't demand divine provision outside of divine alignment. It's not that God plays favorites; it's that His favor follows order.

When we're walking in His will, we walk under the flow of His provision. But when we step out of His will, we step out from under His covering. It's not about striving for blessing; it's about staying close enough to hear His direction.

God Uses What We Think Disqualifies Us
Sometimes we hide what God wants to use because we think it's not good enough. Yet Scripture shows how often He chooses the unlikely: Moses with his stutter, Gideon with his fear, David with his sling, Mary with her youth.

History gives us another glimpse of how God uses what's already in our hands through the life of George Washington Carver. Each morning, Carver would rise before dawn and walk into his laboratory to pray, "Mr. Creator, teach me all about the peanut." That simple prayer of dependence became the doorway to divine revelation.

Carver's curiosity was not ambition; it was intimacy. He believed that if God created the peanut, then God must know its secrets. Through that daily partnership, Carver discovered more than three hundred uses for the peanut and revolutionized agriculture in the South. He later said, "When you do the common things in life in an uncommon way, you will command the attention of the world."

The story of George Washington Carver's life reminds us that More doesn't begin with grandeur; it begins with surrender. Like Carver, when we invite God to breathe on what's in our hands, He transforms the ordinary into the extraordinary. Divine creativity flows through yielded hearts.

"God chose the foolish things of the world to shame the wise; God chose the weak things of the world to shame the strong" (1 Corinthians 1:27). When you yield your weakness to Him, He turns it into strength.

Author and speaker Joyce Meyer once wondered if anyone would listen to her raspy voice. That same voice eventually became her trademark of authority and authenticity. God didn't change her voice; He anointed it.

Maybe your story is your staff. Maybe your compassion or quiet faithfulness is what God wants to magnify. What you see as ordinary may be the very thing Heaven has marked as extraordinary. God often hides greatness in simplicity so that when it's revealed, He alone receives the glory. Your past pain, your hidden gift, or your

---

humble obedience could be the instrument He uses to set others free. Don't underestimate what's in your hand or in your heart. When surrendered to Him, even the smallest offering becomes a vessel of divine power.

We often pray for God to bless our weak areas, but what if He also wants to anoint our strong ones? When you yield *all*—heart, mind, soul, and strength—He doesn't just patch flaws; He ignites your purpose.

When God Expands What's in Your Hand

There was a season when I sat behind a classroom desk, surrounded by lesson plans and the quiet hum of little ones napping nearby, whispering, "Lord, is this all there is?" What I didn't know then was that this question would become an invitation. God wasn't calling me to abandon what was in my hand; He was calling me to *see it differently*.

He took what I thought was ordinary—teaching school—and began to expand it. I followed His nudge toward mathematics and discovered joy in the very thing I'd once resisted. Soon, He opened doors for me to teach computer science, LEGO robotics, coding, and entrepreneurship. I watched children light up as they created things and solved problems.

Later came grants, awards, and eventually the co-founding of a STEM after-school program at our church. Each step was a reminder: God doesn't always move you; He often *expands* you. What began as a whisper of weariness became a story of multiplication.

When God Anoints What You Already Have

God rarely starts with something new; He starts with what's *already in your hand.* What we see as ordinary, He sees as opportunity. When surrendered to Him, the familiar becomes supernatural, the common becomes consecrated, and what once felt small begins to carry kingdom weight.

Example	Transformation
Gideon's fear	Became courage that inspired an army and delivered a nation (Judges 6–7).
Moses' staff	Became a symbol of divine authority that parted seas and demonstrated God's power (Exodus 4).
David's sling	Became a weapon of victory that silenced giants and announced destiny (1 Samuel 17).
Joyce Meyer's voice	Became a global instrument of truth and authenticity that reaches millions.
Your story	Can become someone else's freedom; a testimony that reminds the world that God still redeems.

God doesn't discard the ordinary; He anoints it. He takes what feels insignificant and breathes eternity into it. The very thing you've overlooked or minimized may be the tool He plans to use to change lives. The moment you yield it to Him, it becomes more than a talent; it becomes a touchpoint for His presence.

So, yield your *all*: your intellect, your creativity, your gifts, and even your flaws. In God's hands, your uniqueness becomes your ministry. What you bring isn't just material; it's holy ground. The anointing isn't about adding something new; it's about uncovering what's already there and letting the power of God rest on it.

When you stop trying to perfect what you have and start surrendering it, that's when the miracle begins. Because the same God who anointed a shepherd's sling, a stuttering prophet's staff, and a woman's unpolished voice is still anointing ordinary vessels today—vessels like *you*.

A Coaching Reflection
Pause for a moment and ask:

- What small act of obedience might God be waiting for me to say "yes" to?
- What if the expansion I'm praying for is hidden inside the assignment I already have?
- How might God be asking me to shift from frustration to faithfulness right where I am?

Wholeness leads to purpose, and purpose flows through obedience. You don't need more; you just need to offer what's already in your hand. What God can do with your surrender far exceeds what you could ever accomplish through striving. When you yield what you have—your time, your talent, your story, your scars—He breathes on it and multiplies it. The miracle isn't in how much you hold; it's in how willing you are to release it. When obedience meets availability, Heaven moves through ordinary hands to accomplish extraordinary things.

Once you recognize what's in your hand, lift your eyes because the God who anoints your hands also awakens your vision. The same power that flows through your obedience is the power that opens your eyes to see what's possible with Him. Healing has prepared your heart, purpose has steadied your steps, and now vision will guide your path forward.

God expands our hands through obedience, but He enlarges our world through vision. What He places in your hand is meant to build; what He places in your heart is meant to *behold*. When you begin to see through His eyes, limitation loses its grip. You stop measuring your capacity by your past and start seeing your potential through His promises.

This is where the journey of More deepens—not just doing for God, but seeing with God. He's calling you higher, inviting you to imagine, dream, and step into the unseen future He's already written for you.

As you turn the page, the question shifts. It's no longer only *What's in your hand?* but also *What do you see?* Because the God who gave you purpose is now ready to give you vision, and that's where we're headed next.

Selah: What's in Your Hand?
"Then the LORD said to him, 'What is that in your hand?'" (Exodus 4:2).

There is always something already in your hand—a gift, a skill, a story, a seed—just waiting for God's touch. Like Moses' staff, it may seem ordinary, but when placed in the hands of an extraordinary God, it becomes miraculous. The question is not *What do you lack?* but *What have you overlooked?* It's not about waiting for more; it's about releasing what you already carry.

When gratitude becomes your posture and obedience your rhythm, even the smallest thing can shift nations, heal hearts, and change legacies. Take a deep breath. Look at your hands. What has He already entrusted to you? What ideas, relationships, or experiences has He placed there for such a time as this? Offer them back to Him and watch as He multiplies what you surrender.

Pause & Reflect
- What have I dismissed as too small or too simple?
- How can I honor what I already have with greater faithfulness and gratitude?
- What might God be preparing to release through what I already carry?

Write honestly. Pray deeply. Let His presence steady you as you reflect.

Prayer of Surrender
Father, You are the Giver of every good and perfect gift.

Forgive me for the times I've despised what You've entrusted to me or compared my portion to another's.

Teach me to see the value in the small, the beauty in the simple, and the power in the surrendered.

I place what's in my hand back into Yours.

Anoint it. Multiply it. Use it for Your glory.

In Jesus' name, Amen.

Action Step: Offering What You Have

List three gifts, skills, or passions God has placed in your hand. Dedicate them

> *"Purpose begins with surrender"*

back to Him in prayer, asking, "Lord, use what's in my hand for Your glory." Keep that list visible as a reminder that purpose begins with surrender.

CHAPTER 6

"What Do You See?"
Enlarging Your Vision & Walking by Faith

After God asked Moses, "What is that in your hand?" He taught him to act in faith: "Moreover the word of the LORD came to me, saying, 'Jeremiah, what do you see?' And I said, 'I see a branch of an almond tree.' Then the LORD said to me, 'You have seen well, for I am ready to perform My word'" (Jeremiah 1:11–12 NKJV).

Once we've surrendered what's in our hands, God lifts our eyes to what's ahead. He invites us into a higher conversation—not about our limitations, but about His vision.

The same question whispered to Jeremiah still echoes to us today: *What do you see?* It's more than a question of eyesight; it's a question of insight. God isn't asking for observation but for revelation. He's inviting us to see through the lens of faith, beyond what is visible and into what is possible.

Vision always begins with surrender. When we release what's in our hands, our hearts become free to perceive what He's revealing. And often, the first step toward seeing God's More is believing He wants to show it to us.

You may be standing in a familiar place—same routine, same responsibilities—but with new eyes, that place becomes holy ground. The very setting you once saw as ordinary can become the landscape of destiny when viewed through the Spirit's perspective.

From Hands to Eyes: The Divine Shift

There comes a sacred moment in the journey when God shifts our focus—from our hands to our eyes. First, He calls us to open our hands in surrender and obedience. Then, He lifts our gaze to awaken vision. Because once our hands are freed from fear, comparison, and striving, our eyes can finally see clearly. Only then can we recognize what He's been revealing all along—the next steps, the new possibilities, and the unseen promises waiting to unfold.

Faith gives you a new focal point. It shifts you from *Lord, how?* to *Lord, I see what You're doing.* It moves you from doubt to discernment, from confusion to clarity, from blindness to belief.

Every Woman's Question

Every woman has a moment when the question bubbles up, sometimes in a whisper, sometimes in a cry: *Is this really it? Is this all my life was meant to be?* For me, that moment came in a kindergarten classroom. Lesson plans were piled high, my two youngest children slept on beanbags in the corner, and exhaustion pressed me into the chair like quicksand. I call that stage "entering the pit"—a sinkhole of emptiness. It wasn't that I didn't love my students, my family, or my ministry. I did. But I felt swallowed up by the mundane, caught between gratitude for what I had and a gnawing ache that surely there must be more.

The pit is not failure; it's an invitation. It's the place where God meets us in our emptiness—not to shame us, but to lift our heads toward His fullness. Jesus said in John 10:10, "I have come that they may have life, and have it to the full." That's the More I was aching for—not perfection, but the limitless fullness of Christ.

The Cry for *More*

Before that day in the kindergarten classroom, the ache for More had already begun to take root in my life. Years earlier, when Don and I were just two young people—ages seventeen and eighteen, respectively—trying to make sense of God's call on our lives, He spoke clearly to our hearts. It wasn't through thunder or lightning, but through the quiet conviction that settles deep in your spirit and won't let go.

One night, before a spontaneous young adult prayer service, Don and I were sitting in the car waiting for the church doors to open. The Lord spoke these words to Don, "You will be married a year from August." We had been praying and fasting about God's timing for six weeks that summer.

The timing didn't make sense. We were young and unsure. But His voice was unmistakable. With trembling hearts, we prayed the only prayer we knew: "Lord, show us how." That became our anthem. And true to His word, exactly one year later, we were married to the glory of God.

Similarly, years later, He spoke again: "A year from now, you will plant a church in Atlanta, Georgia." And so, we packed up our car, pregnant with promise— literally and spiritually—and drove nine hundred miles with faith as our map. Exactly one year from the day He spoke, we moved into our home in Atlanta. Eight days later, surrounded by family visiting and eight chairs from Office Max in our empty dining room, we launched our first service on a Sunday evening.

That was the birth of our church. God had done it again. He had taken our small, trembling, "show us how", and turned it into His holy now.

Discovering His *More*

Looking back, I realize God had been preparing me all along. Each "show us how" moment had been a stepping stone to a deeper truth: His More was never about activity; it was about alignment.

When I cried out again from that kindergarten pit, His answer came quietly: "It's not about doing more; it's about discovering My More." That phrase became my lifeline. God wasn't inviting me to add more tasks; He was inviting me to experience Him.

In this season of my life, Paul's words in Ephesians 3:20 came alive: "Now to Him who is able to do immeasurably more than all we ask or imagine, according to His power that is at work within us." The shift was clear:

From performance → presence

From control → trust

From self-reliance → Spirit-dependence

I had mistaken productivity for purpose. God was showing me that fruitfulness flows from intimacy. Real More doesn't come from hustling harder or checking spiritual boxes; it comes from resting in His presence and allowing His Spirit to do the work within you. Intimacy with God becomes the seedbed of vision, creativity, and lasting impact. When you abide in Him, your doing naturally flows from your being. Purpose no longer feels like pressure; it feels like partnership. The peace that once felt elusive begins to grow quietly in the soil of surrender.

A Prayer for Enlargement

A few months later, an opportunity came to lead a summer Bible study. I almost said no, but something in my spirit nudged me: *Say yes.* That six-week study became my classroom of transformation. The book we studied? *The Prayer of Jabez.*

"Oh, that You would bless me and enlarge my territory! Let Your hand be with me, and keep me from harm so that I will be free from pain" (1 Chronicles 4:10). Those words pierced through the fog as God whispered, "This is the prayer you've been aching for." Leading that study wasn't just about me teaching others—it was about God teaching me. He was enlarging my capacity to believe and to see His hand at work.

El Roi: The God Who Sees Me

Before I could truly learn to see through God's eyes, I had to remember: He saw me first. In Genesis 21, Hagar sat in the wilderness, convinced her story was over. Yet in that moment, *El Roi*—the God who sees—opened her eyes to a well that had been there all along. What changed wasn't her situation; it was her sight.

I've been there too—sitting in my own wilderness, hearing that same whisper: "Look again"—when all along, the Lord's provision had been there the entire time. That's what *El Roi* does—He sees us when we can't see our way out, and He helps us to see Him.

The more I prayed, the more my spiritual sight changed. God started teaching me that More isn't about quantity—it's about clarity. When He called Jeremiah, He asked, "What do you see?" (Jeremiah 1:11–12). God trained Jeremiah's eyes before releasing his voice. Before God enlarges our assignment, He enlarges our vision. Elisha prayed for his frightened servant, "Open his eyes, LORD, so that he may see" (2 Kings 6:17). Suddenly, the servant saw the hills filled with horses and chariots of fire.

Vision rarely happens in isolation. Even the most brilliant ideas often need others to bring them to life. The story of Thomas Edison and

Lewis Latimer illustrates this truth. Edison is often remembered as the man who invented the light bulb, but it was Lewis Latimer, the son of formerly enslaved parents, who created the carbon filament that made Edison's invention durable and practical for everyday use. Without Latimer's contribution, Edison's light would have burned out too quickly to illuminate the world.

God often works the same way. One person carries the spark; another carries the sustaining wisdom. Together, they bring forth light that changes lives. That's what partnership looks like in the Kingdom: shared vision, mutual humility, and the understanding that no one shines alone. True vision invites collaboration, because God's light was never meant to be contained in one person's hands.

Anyone can describe what is; faith sees what can be. That's what it means to walk by faith and not by sight. Faith lifts our eyes beyond the visible to the promises of God that have not yet manifested, teaching us to see through His perspective rather than our own limitations.

Faith doesn't deny reality; it redefines it through the lens of God's promises. Where others see lack, faith sees the beginning of provision.

> "Faith doesn't deny reality; it redefines it through the lens of God's promises."

Where others see defeat, faith sees a setup for victory.

Faith lifts your eyes above what's visible and anchors them in what's eternal. It allows you to see beyond the wilderness, beyond the waiting, beyond the walls, and into the wonder of what God is doing behind the scenes. To walk by faith and not by sight is to let God's Word paint your reality instead of your circumstances. It's choosing to see life not as it looks, but as He has spoken it to be.

Enlarging Vision: My Story Continued

That obedience became a turning point. The more I longed for God's more, the more I realized He wasn't moving me; He was expanding me. He led me toward mathematics, a path I hadn't planned. I became a gifted math teacher and later a specials teacher for subjects such as computer science, LEGO robotics, and entrepreneurship. My students built cardboard arcades, created coded sight-word games, and discovered the joy of innovation.

God kept widening my territory: STEM specialist, grant writer, award winner, and eventually co-founder of a STEM after-school program at our church. The funny part? The first Bible study I led after my "pit" moment was *The Prayer of Jabez*. Years after teaching *The Prayer of Jabez*, I realized God was speaking expansion over me the entire time.

He has since expanded my influence in teaching, coaching, and ministry. Every "yes" became an open door; every act of obedience became proof that His More is never about doing—it's about becoming.

A New Season: Coaching and Calling

One radio interview I did became a divine turning point for me. As I spoke, the Holy Spirit whispered Jeremiah 15:19: "If you extract the precious from the worthless, you will become My spokesman" (NASB1995). That word shaped my calling to help others find the treasure in their own stories.

During a coaching session with Pastor Charlene Williams, I asked her, "What do you dream?" She paused, then said softly, "I haven't dreamed since I was ten." Yet as she remembered her childhood desire to write, something awakened inside her. That moment birthed books, teaching opportunities, and a new season of ministry.

That's the power of Spirit-led coaching—to awaken vision where dreams once slept. Each time I speak or coach, I pray: "Lord, help me see and speak like You—to draw out the precious, to call forth purpose, and to remind every heart that You see them." That's what *El Roi* still does—He lets others see Him through us.

You may not be called to teach, lead, or coach, but God is calling you to lift your eyes. Where you see exhaustion, He sees expansion. Where you see limitation, He sees opportunity. Where you see "just another day," He sees a divine assignment.

Maybe, like Pastor Charlene, you stopped dreaming long ago. But dormant dreams still breathe beneath the surface. God is inviting you to look again. He's not asking you to resurrect old plans but to rediscover divine purpose.

You are never too late, too old, or too far gone to dream, because the God who gave you those dreams hasn't forgotten them. He is the One who plants vision in the soil of your spirit and waters it in His perfect season. When God authors a dream, it carries His fingerprints and His timing. Even when life has pressed pause, He never stops preparing.

Sometimes, He lets a dream rest until your heart is ready to carry it. Other times, He resurrects it in a new form, shaped by wisdom, surrender, and grace. The same God who gave Joseph a dream in a prison, and reignited Sarah's hope in her nineties, still breathes life into the visions He's placed within you.

When God opens your eyes, everything changes. You begin to see that His vision was never meant for you to carry alone. The same God who restores your sight also surrounds you with people to help you walk it out: friends, mentors, and

> "When God opens your eyes, everything changes"

encouragers who will steady your hands when the work feels heavy and remind you of what He showed you when life grows dim. Vision awakens destiny, but community sustains it. As we move forward, we'll discover the beauty of divine partnership and what it means to have others who hold up your arms when the calling feels too great to carry alone.

Selah: Lift Your Eyes

"And God opened her eyes, and she saw a well of water" (Genesis 21:19 KJV).

There are moments when God doesn't change our surroundings; He changes our sight. Like Hagar in the wilderness, we sit weary and uncertain, believing our story is finished. But *El Roi*, the God who sees us, gently whispers, "Look again."

When God opens your eyes, you begin to see what has been there all along—His provision, His purpose, His presence. The pit becomes a passage. The desert reveals a well. The ordinary becomes divine.

The God who sees you, *El Roi*, has never lost sight of you. When you lift your eyes from what's been lost or delayed, you'll find that His provision, His purpose, and His presence have been beside you all along.

This chapter invited you to see beyond what is and believe again in what can be. God isn't asking you to dream the same dreams you once had; He's inviting you to see them through His eyes, this time with faith instead of fear, with hope instead of hesitation.

Look again. What seemed like a wilderness may actually be the well He prepared for you. What felt like an ending might just be the beginning of something new. When you allow God to restore your sight, He renews your strength, your purpose, and your hope.

Take a deep breath. Pause and pray. Let Heaven adjust your focus.

Pause & Reflect
- Where have I mistaken the pit for the end instead of an invitation to deeper purpose?
- What dream or desire might God be telling me to look at again?
- Where is God enlarging my vision and asking me to trust His view over my own?
- What's my "Show me how, Lord" prayer in this season?

Write honestly. Pray deeply. Let His presence steady you as you reflect.

Prayer of Vision
Father, thank You for being El Roi—*the God who sees me.*

Lift my eyes beyond fear, fatigue, or failure.

Open my heart to perceive Your presence where I once saw only problems.

Teach me to look again, to dream again, and to see through Heaven's lens.

Expand my faith to match the future You've prepared.

I yield my sight to Your Spirit.

In Jesus' name, Amen.

Action Step: Offering What You Have
List three gifts, skills, or passions God has placed in your hand.

Dedicate them back to Him in prayer, asking, "Lord, use what's in my hand for Your glory." Keep that list visible as a reminder that purpose begins with surrender.

Vision Declaration I will not live by what I see—I will live by faith. I will see promise where others see impossibility. I will look again until my vision aligns with His word. My eyes are fixed on the God of More, And I am ready to see all He has prepared for me.

Will You Remember? When God restores your sight, He doesn't just show you the future; He reminds you of His faithfulness in the past. Now that your eyes are open, it's time to remember what you've seen—because remembrance is the bridge between revelation and legacy.

E — EMBRACE THE MORE LIFE

Living out God's fullness in community, wholeness, purpose, and legacy

*"I have come that they may have life, and that they may have it **more abundantly**."*
JOHN 10:10 (NKJV)

CHAPTER 7

"Will You Remember?"

The Power of Experiences — Good and Bad — to Shape the More Life

"Remember how the LORD your God led you all the way in the wilderness these forty years, to humble and test you in order to know what was in your heart." (Deuteronomy 8:2)

L ife is a story made of moments; some we want to replay forever, and others we wish we could erase. But God's Word is clear: *Both matter.* Both the blessings and the battles shape who we are and who we are becoming. That's why Deuteronomy 8:2 reminds us, "Remember how the LORD your God led you all the way in the wilderness these forty years, to humble and test you in order to know what was in your heart."

God doesn't waste wilderness seasons. He doesn't waste victories either. The command to remember is a command to *notice* His hand in it all.

Memory is not passive; it's spiritual. To *remember* in Scripture (Hebrew: *zakar*) means more than to recall; it means to recall with intention and gratitude. When God "remembered" Noah, Hannah, or Israel, He acted in compassion and covenant love.

The question for us is this: *Will you remember what God has done in your life, not just the good, but also the places you'd rather forget?*

Because your experiences, both painful and beautiful, can become the very soil where legacy is planted.

Stones of Remembrance

When Israel crossed the Jordan River into the Promised Land, God gave them a curious command. He told Joshua to have one man from each tribe pick up a stone from the riverbed.

> *"God doesn't waste wilderness seasons. He doesn't waste victories either. The command to remember is a command to notice His hand in it all."*

When they reached the other side, they piled the twelve stones together as a memorial.

Joshua explained: "In the future, when your children ask you, 'What do these stones mean?' tell them that the flow of the Jordan was cut off before the ark of the covenant of the LORD. ... These stones are to be a memorial to the people of Israel forever" (Joshua 4:6–7).

Why stones? Because stones endure. Long after the people forgot the details, the stones would still speak.

Your life experiences, both the miraculous crossings and the painful wildernesses, are *stones of remembrance*. They are memorials of what God has brought you through. And one day, when your children or grandchildren ask, "What do these stones mean?" you'll be able to tell them:

This is where God carried me.

This is where He made a way.

This is where His grace held me together.

Every stone is a sermon. Every scar, a sacred reminder that His hand was faithful when yours was trembling.

The Lessons of Suffering

Some stones, like as answered prayers, breakthroughs, and victories, are easy to celebrate. Others feel too heavy to lift: the losses, the disappointments, and the griefs that still sting.

> "your experiences, both painful and beautiful, can become the very soil where legacy is planted."

Job knew that weight. After all his suffering, God didn't give him tidy answers. Instead, He asked, "Where were you when I laid the earth's foundation?" (Job 38:4). It wasn't cruelty; it was *perspective*. God was reminding Job that his pain was not the whole story. Job's perspective was limited, but God's was eternal.

I experienced this paradox in one of the hardest weeks of my life. It was 2020, and I had just been named Teacher of the Year—one of the greatest professional honors I'd ever received. In that very same week, my mother passed away. Grief and celebration collided in a way I didn't know was possible.

> "Every stone is a sermon. Every scar, a sacred reminder that His hand was faithful when yours was trembling."

One moment, I was standing in the glow of recognition. Next, I was standing at my mother's grave.

How do you hold both?

I remember feeling like I couldn't breathe, like joy and sorrow were pulling me apart in opposite directions. And yet, God met me there. He taught me that sometimes life is not either/or; it's both/and. Sometimes the stones we carry are both *heavy and holy*.

And even in that, He is present.

Remembering doesn't mean pretending the pain doesn't hurt. It means recognizing that God is still weaving His purposes through it. It's understanding that *the same God who stood with you in your victory will sit with you in your valley.*

Sometimes, the greatest act of faith is simply to say: "I will remember."

Do You See This Woman?
In Luke 7, Jesus is dining at a Pharisee's house when a woman bursts in, a woman everyone in town knows by her reputation. She kneels at Jesus' feet, weeping, washing His feet with her tears and drying them with her hair.

The religious leaders are scandalized. But Jesus says something that still takes my breath away: "Do you see this woman?" (Luke 7:44).

They saw her sin. He saw her story.

They saw shame. He saw worship.

That moment became her testimony. Her experiences, the broken ones, the shame-filled ones, were not wasted. In the presence of Jesus, they became redeemed.

And isn't that true for us, too? Our hardest experiences can become altars of worship. Our shame can become our song of grace. Our brokenness can become our boldness. We remember not to relive our failures, but to reveal His faithfulness.

Turning Experiences into Testimonies

Romans 8:28 is not a cliché; it's a lifeline: "And we know that in all things God works for the good of those who love Him, who have been called according to His purpose."

Notice it doesn't say *all things are good*. Some experiences are deeply painful, unjust, or tragic. But in *all* things, God is working.

This is where I think of the Japanese art of *kintsugi*. When pottery breaks, artisans don't throw it away. They mend the cracks with gold. The vessel becomes more beautiful, more valuable, because of where it was broken.

That is what God does with our experiences. He doesn't erase the cracks; He fills them with His glory. And those very cracks become the most powerful part of your testimony.

When you choose to remember through the lens of grace, you can look at your scars and say:

This is where God healed me.

This is where His strength carried me.

This is where His light shone through my weakness.

Your experiences, good and bad, are not wasted. They are gold-filled cracks, shimmering reminders of God's faithfulness.

Scars, Wounds, and Stones of Remembrance

Not all experiences feel complete. Some are *scars*, healed places that remain visible reminders of where we've been. Others are *open wounds*, tender and raw, needing the Father's touch. Scars tell a story. They are like memorial stones in our own bodies and souls, reminding us of battles fought and victories won. Paul bore what

---

he called "the marks of Jesus" (Galatians 6:17). His scars weren't shameful; they were sacred. They testified to God's faithfulness through suffering.

But wounds that remain open, like scabs we keep picking at, cannot heal. They fester with bitterness, anger, or grief. And those wounds cannot become memorial stones until they are lifted before the Father.

Pain is the body's way of getting our attention, a sign that something needs healing. In the same way, spiritual pain is God's way of drawing us back to Himself. Pain is not meant to be ignored; it's an *invitation* to bring our hurt into His presence so He can heal what festers and transform it into testimony.

We will not understand all things on this side of eternity. As Paul wrote, "For now we see only a reflection as in a mirror; then we shall see face to face." (1 Corinthians 13:12)

For now, we trust. We trust that one day, when we stand before Him, the threads will make sense, the tapestry will become clear, and the gold in the cracks will shine with His glory. Until then, we bring our wounds to the Father for healing and let our scars become testimony stones that say: *Here is where He carried me. Here is where His love held me together. Here is where His grace turned pain into purpose.*

Experiences as Sacred Training

It's easy to dismiss our ordinary experiences as unspiritual things like teaching classrooms, managing homes, or running businesses. Yet in Scripture, God often used *experience* as the training ground for destiny:

- Joseph's betrayal, slavery, and imprisonment became preparation for leadership in Egypt.
- David's lonely nights with sheep became rehearsal for courage before Goliath.
- Daniel, Shadrach, Meshach, and Abednego learned influence in Babylon before they faced hungry lions or stood in the furnace.
- Paul's tentmaking gave him credibility to minister among working people.
- The disciples' fishing nets became their classroom for learning how to "fish for men."

God is the Master Teacher. Nothing in your story is wasted. Every experience—the pit, the palace, the prison, the pulpit—is shaping you for the More Life. Even your detours are divine directions in disguise.

Remembering as Worship

Remembering is not just reflection; it is worship.

When the psalmist says, "Praise the LORD, my soul, and forget not all His benefits" (Psalm 103:2), he's not suggesting a mental exercise but a spiritual posture. To "forget not" is to *anchor your faith in the history of His faithfulness.*

In the Old Testament, worship and remembrance were always intertwined. The Passover meal was a yearly act of remembering God's deliverance. And at the Last Supper, Jesus said,

"Do this in remembrance of Me" (Luke 22:19). Why? Because forgetfulness leads to fear, but remembrance restores faith.

Every time we pause to remember what God has done; we build an altar of gratitude that guards our hearts against despair.

Remembering trains us to see His hand even in the hidden places. So, when you look back over your life—your wilderness, your Jordan crossings, your scars, and your songs—see them not as random scenes but as *rehearsals of grace*.

Our experiences, both painful and beautiful, are never wasted. They become the stones we set up for generations to see, the scars that tell of His healing, the *kintsugi* cracks where His glory shines.

But legacy is not built on experiences alone. If we're honest, some of those experiences would have crushed us had it not been for the people God placed in our lives. When we were too weak to pray, they prayed. When we were too weary to stand, they stood beside us. When we wanted to quit, they reminded us of the call.

Because the More Life is not meant to be lived in isolation. It is woven together in the fabric of community, in the hands that lift ours when they fall, in the voices that call out the More in us when we can't see it ourselves.

So, after asking the question *Will you remember?* we must now ask another: *Who holds up your arms?*

Selah: Remember and Rejoice

"Remember how the LORD your God led you all the way in the wilderness these forty years, to humble and test you in order to know what was in your heart" (Deuteronomy 8:2).

There are sacred moments in our journey when God calls us to pause — to look back and see His fingerprints over every season, the wilderness and the wonder alike. Remembering isn't about reliving pain or regret; it's about recognizing His faithfulness.

Every trial that tested you, every tear that shaped you, every triumph that strengthened you— they are all part of your story of becoming. These moments become stones of remembrance, sacred markers of the God who led, sustained, and never left your side.

Take a moment to breathe deeply, reflect prayerfully, and rejoice in the faithfulness of the Lord who has carried you this far.

Pause & Reflect

- What experience from my past still feels unfinished, and how might God want to redeem it?
- Where have I allowed pain to rename me instead of letting God redefine me?
- What memorial stones, or moments of His faithfulness, can I set up to remember what God has done?
- What lessons has God taught me in wilderness seasons that I don't want to forget?
- Who needs to hear the story of how God has revealed His faithfulness in my life?

Write honestly. Pray deeply. Let His presence steady you as you reflect.

Prayer of Remembrance & Gratitude

Lord, help me to remember.

Don't let me forget Your faithfulness in my wilderness—

in the triumphs and in the trials.

Thank You for every season that shaped me,

every lesson that humbled me,

and every blessing that reminded me You were with me all along.

Take every experience—good and bad—and weave it into testimony.

Fill my cracks with Your glory, and let my life become a living memorial stone

that points others to Your steadfast love and faithfulness.

Amen.

My Stones of Remembrance
List key moments, miracles, or lessons where you've seen God's hand at work.

1. _____
2. _____
3. _____
4. _____
5. _____

Action Step: A Visible Reminder of God's Faithfulness
Choose one moment in your life where you clearly saw God's hand—through provision, healing, guidance, or restoration. Write it on a stone, note card, or journal page and label it "My Memorial Stone." Place it somewhere you'll see it often. Each time you look at it, pause to thank God for His faithfulness and whisper, *"You were faithful then, and You are faithful still."*

CHAPTER 8
"Who Holds Up Your Arms?"
Strength in Community & the Power of Partnership

"When Moses' hands grew tired, they took a stone and put it under him, and he sat on it. Aaron and Hur held his hands up—one on one side, one on the other—so that his hands remained steady till sunset" (Exodus 17:12).

There was a Sunday when Don and I were ready to quit ministry. We had poured ourselves out for others, only to feel misunderstood, criticized, and alone. That day, it felt like we were the enemy in our own church. The exhaustion and disappointment pressed on us so heavily that at one point, Don stood up and announced that he was done pastoring.

I sat there silently, feeling broken, not arguing or defending—just empty. But God had other plans. During that very service, two men quietly stepped forward. They didn't make grand speeches or offer solutions; they simply said they would stand with us and hold up our arms. Within a week, a woman who hadn't been in that service came to me after hearing what had happened and told me she would hold up my arms too.

Those three people served us with their steady hands and faithful hearts, showing up when challenges came, helping us navigate trials, and standing with us as the foundation of the church was laid and strengthened.

Years later, during another season of testing when our son Brandon became ill, church members once again surrounded us in love. They volunteered to bring meals, cut our grass, and even repair the tiles in our foyer. Their hands and hearts helped us stay steady through that storm.

Looking back, I know that if those people hadn't obeyed God's nudge to step up, we might have walked away. They became our Aarons and Hurs, holding up our arms when we no longer had the strength to lift them ourselves.

Ministry Was Never Meant to Be Carried Alone

Community is where healing happens. The More Life was never meant to be lived in isolation. Ironically, although we live in a hyperconnected world, human beings are lonelier than ever. According to the U.S. Surgeon General, about one in two adults in America reports feeling lonely on a regular basis. Despite thousands of followers online, hearts are starving for real connection.

In his 2023 advisory, the U.S. Surgeon General described loneliness and isolation as an epidemic, noting that about half of adults in America experience loneliness. The Church is not immune. The Barna Group , in a 2022 study, reported that 42 percent of pastors had considered quitting full-time ministry in the past year, citing burnout, isolation, and emotional exhaustion as primary causes.

"Community is where healing happens."

Lifeway Research confirms a similar reality in its 2023 article "Debunking the Myths: Ministry Burnout and Leaving the Ministry," which highlights that while many pastors remain deeply committed to their calling, they often do so under immense personal strain. The study notes that burnout doesn't always mean a loss of faith; it often signals a loss of community, rest, and support. In other words, even strong leaders can't sustain ministry alone.

Don and I learned that truth the hard way. After visiting Saddleback Church in California years ago and learning from Pastor Rick Warren about The Purpose Driven Life, we realized that our church, and we ourselves, needed deeper fellowship with like-minded believers. In 2002, we began implementing small-group ministry, and over time, the culture of our church changed. The weight of ministry pressure began to lighten. There will always be resistance to the call of Jesus Christ, but the load feels lighter when others are lifting it with you.

We've been blessed with support from our bishop and his wife, from fellow pastors, elders, and friends who share not only ministry conversations but life itself. We belong to small groups, protect our family time, and carve out space for one another as husband and wife. Ministry will always involve sacrifice, but boundaries ensure that our first ministry, our family, remains a priority.

This year, our church celebrated thirty-one years of ministry, and Don and I celebrated thirty-seven years of marriage. Our children are grown, married, and have given us the gift of four beautiful grandchildren with two on the way. What a joy it is to be able to pour into them and to experience the fruit of faithfulness through the generations.

We've learned to build rhythms that keep us grounded: community, rest, and accountability. We fellowship with other pastors, travel with friends, and intentionally step away to recharge. Last year, we spent a month visiting the beautiful nations of Ghana and South Africa. It was a journey that reminded us that even shepherds need still waters. Ministry may be a calling, but it was never meant to be a solo assignment.

The Gift of Godly Friendship: Pastor Kameshia

Some of the greatest miracles God performs come wrapped in friendship. I met Pastor Kameshia Stokes Thomas at a pastors' wives retreat hosted by our spiritual mother, Dr. Nina Bronner. The retreat was held at a cozy farmhouse in South Georgia and was a gathering for women who were married to pastors under Bishop Dale Bronner's leadership.

The first time Pastor Kameshia and I met, I didn't think she liked me. During our group discussions, I kept interjecting my opinion and answering the questions she was directing at Dr. Nina. She got so annoyed with me. She was right—I kept butting in! What she didn't know was that I felt like an outsider at that gathering. It was my first time attending, and I assumed everyone else already knew each other. I was nervous and guarded, carrying a few scars from ministry.

But those retreats were life-giving. Dr. Nina modeled such warmth and wisdom. She would make fresh vegetable juices in the morning, and on occasion, I'd cook waffles for everyone. When we arrived at each location, there were always fresh flowers, a candle, and a thoughtful little gift waiting in our rooms. It felt like home, a space where we could breathe and just be women, not "the pastor's wife."

Each year, Dr. Nina would take us somewhere different in Georgia: Callaway Gardens, Amicalola Falls, the mountains, or a lake house. We'd laugh, pray, and learn from one another. It wasn't long before I decided that if she or Bishop ever invited us again, my answer would always be "yes." Those retreats became sacred for me—a much-anticipated rhythm of rest and renewal. They reminded me that even women in ministry need a place to lay down the weight of titles and expectations.

It was six months after one of those retreats when Kameshia called me and asked if I'd be her prayer partner. I was surprised—we hadn't spoken much since that first meeting. Later, she told me that during one of our prayer sessions at the retreat, she looked up to see who was softly singing, "Lord, I am available to You," and the Holy Spirit told her that I was to be her prayer partner.

At the time, I was pouring my heart out to God, feeling like I didn't have the luxury of lingering in His presence because I worked full-time. That lie had weighed heavily on me until His Spirit lifted it. That was October 2011. In April 2012, I said "yes" to being Kameshia's prayer partner. I didn't know that "yes" would change my life for the next twelve years. We prayed together weekly, sharing our struggles and celebrating every victory. What started as prayer lists became a living record of God's faithfulness: praise reports, answered prayers, and deeper friendship.

I watched God use Kameshia's humor, wisdom, and grace to impact so many lives. Behind her laughter and comedic "alter-ego," Erma Lee, was a woman of strength and faith. We prayed through her first women's tea, her church anniversaries, and the birth of her grandchildren. She prayed for me through my children's engagements and marriages, professional milestones—like when I was nominated for Teacher of the Year multiple times before finally receiving it—and painful seasons like when my mother passed away. She was even there in the audience when my family competed on *Family Feud*, laughing and cheering louder than anyone else.

When Pastor Kameshia became ill in 2024, I was blessed to see her one last time before her passing: to pray with her, sing softly over her, and kiss her forehead. When I began to sing, she called out my name, letting me know she knew I was there.

What began as two women praying together became a deep, sacred friendship. Kameshia truly held up my arms. When I wanted to shrink back, she would say, "You always act like this right before

God elevates you." Everyone needs a friend like that, a spiritual mirror reflecting the More inside you when you can't see it yourself.

The Power of S.E.A.: Support, Encouragement, Accountability
In my coaching work, I often use the acronym S.E.A. (*Support, Encouragement, Accountability*). Everyone needs these three things if they are going to live the More Life:

- *Support* reminds you that you're not alone. It's the steadying hand that helps you stand when life feels heavy.
- *Encouragement* breathes courage into a weary soul. It's the gentle reminder that your calling still matters and your story isn't over.
- *Accountability* keeps you aligned with your purpose when distractions and detours arise. It's love with structure: a commitment to growth that guards your focus and fuels your faith.

Together, these three form a kind of spiritual ecosystem. When you're surrounded by people who support, encourage, and lovingly hold you accountable, you flourish. Isolation stifles, but connection strengthens. God never designed us to grow in solitude; He designed us to grow in community.

The temptation to hide in plain sight is greater than ever. Because of social media, we can curate our strengths, rather than be seen in our weaknesses. We accept highlight reels in place of heart-level relationships. We scroll for validation instead of reaching for connection. But the More Life calls us to step away from filtered living and step back into authentic, Christ-centered relationships.

Jesus didn't call disciples to be distant followers; He called them to be *friends*. He wept with them, ate with them, laughed with them, and sent them out two by two. That's the model: shared life, shared mission, shared love.

When you have a circle that carries you through storms, prays for you when you're weary, and reminds you of who you are when you forget, you begin to taste the rhythm of heaven on earth. The More Life doesn't just happen in solitude: it grows in S.E.A., where your soul is surrounded by those who lift, steady, and sharpen you.

Holding Up Your Pastor's Arms
Practical Ways to Support Spiritual Leaders

- Pray daily for your pastor and their family.
- Offer help without being asked: meals, errands, repairs, or childcare.
- Encourage often, especially after sermons. Right after a pastor preaches is one of their most vulnerable moments. Speak life. Don't bring complaints; bring gratitude.
- Protect their rest. Respect their Sabbath and family time.
- Celebrate wins—both spiritual and personal.
- Create safe spaces for honest conversations.
- Send notes of gratitude.
- Model unity. Don't gossip. Division drains, harmony heals.
- Give generously. Your giving sustains ministry and fuels purpose.
- Show up in person, not just online, if physically able. God's plan for His body is connection, not isolation.

The Hidden Loneliness of Pastors' Wives

Pastors' wives are often among the loneliest in the congregation, loved yet misunderstood, surrounded yet unseen. As Megan Hill notes, even elders' wives, those in visible ministry, can quietly carry the ache of loneliness. They carry silent burdens, frequently give up their privacy, and often sacrifice personal dreams for the sake of ministry.

A 2016 survey conducted by the Ethics & Religious Liberty Commission found that more than half of pastors' wives feel disconnected or isolated, and 69 percent say they need more time and attention devoted to friendships and fellowship with others. Many reported that they felt unable to confide in anyone within their church because of past betrayals or fears that their honesty would be misunderstood or misused. One woman summarized it poignantly: "We are known by many but deeply known by few."

Christine Hoover, author of *Messy Beautiful Friendship* and a pastor's wife herself, expressed this same reality when she wrote, "The deepest truth is that what I really want is friendship. I'm surrounded by lovely people and countless relationships, but relationships don't always equate to friendship, and I tend to forget that."

When I began my coaching practice, it was birthed from that same ache, from the isolation, loneliness, and unspoken expectations I once carried as a pastor's wife and associate pastor. God called me to reach women who lead, love, and serve quietly in the background, to remind them that He sees them too. That became my heartbeat and niche: ministering to women in ministry who pour out constantly yet rarely feel poured into.

Many pastors' wives serve tirelessly both inside and outside the church, often volunteering countless hours without compensation.

Considering that the average church size in America is fewer than two hundred members, the reality for many women is one of juggling ministry, family, and outside work, with little help or rest. But loneliness doesn't disappear in larger ministries; it simply takes on a different form.

In larger congregations, pastors' wives may appear to have vibrant social circles, staff support, and resources, but looks can be deceiving. The pressures are different, but just as heavy. Many feel the weight of constant visibility, the pressure to perform perfection, or the exhaustion of meeting endless expectations. Their calendars may be full, but their hearts can still be empty. For some, the loneliness is magnified by the lack of safe spaces to be vulnerable without fear of judgment, gossip, or comparison.

The truth is, whether you are part of a small congregation or a megachurch, the ache for authentic connection is the same. Behind every polished smile may be a weary heart longing for a friend who sees beyond the title.

But here's what I've also learned: Not everyone can be your pastor's or your pastor's wife's best friend. Their calling is to love and lead the whole body, not to carry everyone's emotional expectations. Many young pastors' wives have been hurt by misplaced trust or unrealistic demands. You don't need to be their closest friend to show genuine love. Pray for them. Support them. Encourage them without expecting anything in return. That's true ministry.

Their husbands and children carry the weight of the call alongside them. The best way you can love them is to give them space to be human: to rest, to grow, to make mistakes. Let their children be regular kids, loved in grace, not scrutiny. I'm so grateful our church family allowed our children to grow and know Jesus in an atmosphere of love. Today, all of them and their spouses serve the

Lord faithfully. That is the fruit of growing up in a healthy, grace-filled community.

That's why I've begun mentoring and coaching other pastors' wives, to remind them that they are not invisible. They are vital. They are seen by God, loved by their families, and needed by the body of Christ. We, too, need community. A recent study on pastors' wives and mental health confirms what many of us have lived: Ministry is meaningful but can be mentally and emotionally taxing. Because even those who serve from the front need arms that hold them up when the weight of ministry becomes too heavy to carry alone.

The Beauty of "One Another"

Scripture contains over five hundred "one another" commands, including "love one another," "pray for one another," "serve one another," and "forgive one another." Our vertical relationship with God flourishes only when our horizontal relationships are healthy.

We need each other. We sharpen, stretch, and sanctify one another through fellowship, forgiveness, and faith. The More Life is not a solo pursuit; it's a symphony of souls walking together in rhythm with the Spirit.

We were never meant to walk this journey alone. Whether in marriage, ministry, friendship, or faith, God designed us to grow in community: supported,

> *"The More Life is not a solo pursuit; it's a symphony of souls walking together in rhythm with the Spirit."*

encouraged, and strengthened by others who help us see Him more clearly. Each relationship, each person, is part of the divine tapestry He's weaving through our lives.

But ultimately, the question isn't just about who walks beside you. It's about what you'll do with the life God has entrusted to you. Every conversation, every act of service, every moment of surrender becomes part of your legacy.

You've laid down the lies, chosen trust over fear, walked toward healing, and learned the power of community. Now the call deepens. What will you do with the strength, wisdom, and grace God has poured into you?

The people God places around us help shape who we become, but the greater question remains: *What will you do with the life you've been given?* In the next chapter, we'll explore what it means to

> "We were never meant to walk this journey alone. Each relationship is a thread in the divine tapestry God is weaving through our lives."

leave a legacy: to live the More Life not just for ourselves, but for generations to come. Because the More Life is never meant to stop with you; it's meant to flow through you.

Selah: The Gift of Community

"Two are better than one, because they have a good return for their labor: If either of them falls down, one can help the other up" (Ecclesiastes 4:9–10).

There are sacred moments in our journey when we realize we were never meant to walk alone. From the very beginning, God designed community as the place where His love is both given and received. It's in the holding up of weary arms, the shared tears, the laughter, the prayer circles, and the daily encouragement that His Kingdom becomes visible on earth.

The beauty of community is that it reflects the very nature of God Himself: Father, Son, and Holy Spirit, three in perfect unity. When we stand together in faith, we mirror that divine fellowship. When we serve and support one another, we strengthen the bond that keeps us standing when life feels heavy.

The More Life is never lived in isolation; it is cultivated through connection. True wholeness grows where Support, Encouragement, and Accountability (S.E.A.) flow freely between hearts committed to Christ. Take a moment to pause and breathe in gratitude for the people who have walked beside you: those who have prayed for you, held your arms up, and refused to let you fall. Then ask God to show you who *you* are called to strengthen in this season.

Pause & Reflect
- Who has held up your arms when you felt weary? Who are you holding up in return?
- Where do you need to re-engage in community, friendship, or service?
- How can you build a rhythm of S.E.A. (Support, Encouragement, and Accountability) in your life today?

Write honestly. Pray deeply. Let His presence steady you as you reflect.

Prayer of Connection
Father, thank You for the people who have stood beside me when I felt weak,

and for those You've called me to strengthen in return.

Teach me to live in unity: with open hands, open heart, and open eyes to the needs around me.

Help me to cultivate relationships that reflect Your love and build Your Kingdom.

Let my life be a bridge that connects others to You.

In Jesus' name, Amen.

Action Step: Strength in Community
Write down the names of three people who have helped you stand when life felt heavy—those who have prayed for you, encouraged you, or simply showed up. Send each one a note of thanks or a word of encouragement this week. Then, pray and ask God to show you *whose arms you're called to hold up* in this season.

CHAPTER 9

"How Will You Be Remembered?"
Walking in the More Life: A Legacy of Faith & Impact

"What is your life? You are a mist that appears for a little while and then vanishes." (James 4:14)

"Teach us to number our days, that we may gain a heart of wisdom." (Psalm 90:12)

Life is brief. Too brief to waste. When our story is told, it will be marked by a single dash, one line between two dates: the day we were born and the day we leave this world. That dash is small, yet it holds everything—every yes and every no, every sacrifice, every hidden act of love, every whispered prayer. That dash is your legacy.

I often picture life as a tapestry. Up close, it looks like tangled knots and frayed threads. But when you step back, a design emerges, a pattern only the Weaver could see from the start. What once felt random or broken becomes purposeful in His hands.

Or think of *kintsugi*, the Japanese art of repairing broken pottery with gold. The cracks don't disappear; they shine. They become the most valuable part. That's legacy too—not perfection, but redemption. Not flawless lives but surrendered ones that let God's glory shine through every scar.

The dash between your dates may be short, but heaven measures not its length, only its light. The question is not *how long* you live, but *how you will be remembered*.

Why Legacy Matters

Legacy is not about titles, wealth, or accomplishments. It's about faith handed down. Paul reminded Timothy of "your sincere faith, which first lived in your grandmother Lois and in your mother Eunice and, I am persuaded, now lives in you also" (2 Timothy 1:5). That faith didn't end with them; it lived on through him. That's the kind of legacy that outlasts us—not just memories, but a living inheritance of faith, courage, and love.

As Rick Warren is often quoted as saying, "When you die, there are two questions God will ask you: What did you do with My Son, Jesus Christ? And what did you do with what I gave you?"

The first question determines your eternity. The second defines your legacy. Both hinge on stewardship—what you did with your time, your talents, your relationships, and your faith.

The More Life is about living so intentionally that what you leave behind keeps pointing others to the God who is more than enough. Earthly success fades quickly. Recognition passes. But spiritual inheritance multiplies.

The story of faith doesn't stop with you; it keeps unfolding through every person who is touched by your obedience. A legacy anchored in Christ outlives trends, outlasts pain, and outshines titles. It's written not in ink, but in lives changed by love.

A Series of Yeses

I've learned that legacy isn't built in one grand moment. It's built through a lifetime of small yeses.

Yes to God's call when it felt bigger than me.

Yes to the Spirit's whisper when it interrupted my plans.

Yes to marriage at a young age, believing God was in it.

Yes to moving to Atlanta to plant a church when the future was uncertain.

Yes to teaching math and science after the "pit" moment, discovering that God wasn't moving me—He was expanding me.

Yes to coaching, writing, speaking, mentoring, and equipping others to walk in purpose.

Each yes became a thread in a tapestry of surrender. But every yes cost something. Sometimes it cost comfort. Sometimes it cost applause. Sometimes it cost tears I didn't tell anyone about. Yet every yes was an echo of obedience recorded by heaven. Faithful obedience, especially in hidden places, is what shapes a life that lasts. Lott Carey, one of the first African American missionaries, once said: "I am an instrument for the Lord to use." His words echo the heartbeat of legacy. One yes can ripple through generations.

Think about it: Mary's yes brought Christ into the world. Ruth's yes carried redemption into the lineage of Jesus. Esther's yes preserved her nation. Your yes may not be public, but it is powerful. Every surrendered yes becomes a seed that outlives the sower.

The Power of Experiences in Legacy
Think back over your journey: the victories and valleys, the scars and the songs, the answered prayers and the ones that seemed silent. Legacy is not formed *in spite of* those moments but *because of* them.

Your scars become testimony stones for your children.

Your perseverance becomes courage for those who follow.

Your worship in the storm becomes a roadmap for someone else's faith.

Nothing is wasted when it's surrendered. God redeems even the cracks, filling them with gold so His light can shine through—like Dorcas in Acts 9, whose kindness caused widows to weep when she died. Her legacy lived on in the garments she made and the hearts she touched. When Peter prayed and she was raised, it was as if heaven confirmed: *A life that blesses others never truly ends.*

I've seen this truth unfold again and again. Every woman who mentors another is passing the torch of faith. Every mother who prays for her child, every teacher who sows into her students, every pastor who keeps preaching through pain—they are all building eternal stories.

I think of the women in my own life whose prayers became bridges.

My mother, who taught me strength through perseverance and modeled grace, elegance, beauty, and generosity under pressure—strength wrapped in gentleness.

My mother-in-love, who taught me the healing power of joy, who could laugh even in the midst of her sorrow, and reminded me that laughter, too, is a language of faith.

My aunt and godmother, Mary Alice, whose steady presence has carried me through the years, from the loss of my father to every milestone since, showing up with quiet faithfulness and love that never wavered.

My mentors, who called forth gifts I didn't see in myself. Their faith still whispers to me in moments of doubt. That's the power of legacy—it outlives your voice, but it never stops speaking.

Legacy isn't built in applause; it's built in authenticity. People don't remember perfection; they remember presence. They remember who showed up, who cared, who prayed, who stayed.

Living Bigger Than Yourself

Legacy requires living for something greater than yourself. It means asking daily: *How will what I do today outlast me?* Sometimes it looks like starting a ministry, mentoring students, or writing down prayers for your children. Sometimes it looks like choosing integrity when no one's watching or forgiveness when bitterness would be easier.

Legacy grows wherever obedience roots deeply. It's refusing to live small when God has called you to live More. You don't have to have a stage to have significance. You simply have to live surrendered.

When you choose faith over fear, humility over pride, love over resentment, you are laying spiritual stones that will outlast generations. Every ordinary day is an opportunity to build eternal impact. The words you speak, the prayers you whisper, the love you give—all of it counts. Jesus modeled this perfectly. He poured into twelve, who then poured into others. By the world's measure, His ministry was small. But His obedience changed eternity.

No one builds a legacy alone. Those who held up your arms, believed in you, or prayed for you all left fingerprints on your story. And your fingerprints now rest on others. Every time you encourage, mentor, or love, you're etching eternity into someone else's heart.

Legacy multiplies through relationships, through people who glimpse Jesus because of how you serve and how you love. Moses needed Aaron and Hur. Ruth needed Naomi. Paul needed Timothy. Each relationship carried faith forward to the next generation.

The question isn't: *Who made my life easier?* The real question is: *Whose life is lighter because I showed up?* Legacy is less about your name being remembered and more about *His name* being revealed through your life.

Living for the Two Questions

When I think about Rick Warren's two questions: "What did you do with Jesus?" and "What did you do with what He gave you?" I'm reminded that one day our lives will be weighed, not by applause, but by obedience. These two questions, first presented in *The Purpose Driven Life*, capture the essence of eternal perspective. Did we know God and make Him known? Did we invest the gifts He placed in our hands, or did we bury them out of fear?

Jesus told a parable about servants who had been entrusted with talents. Each one received something, different in measure, but equal in opportunity. The master's commendation wasn't for perfection but for faithfulness: "Well done, good and faithful servant!" (Matthew 25:21).

Faithfulness in small things is never wasted. The unseen yeses, the hidden prayers, the quiet sacrifices—they echo louder in eternity than any spotlight ever could. The kingdom of God advances not through the noise of ambition but through the humility of obedience.

The day will come when the applause fades and the lights dim, but heaven's audience remains. And if your life has reflected His love, if your words have carried His truth, if your heart has trusted His plan, you will hear the sweetest sound of all: *Well, done!*

A Call to Rise

This is the invitation of the More Life:

To live not merely for today, but for eternity.

To say yes when it's hard.

To let your scars shine with gold.

To lift others even as you are lifted.

Every act of love, every yes to God, every moment of surrender, is a thread in a legacy that heaven remembers.

Legacy is the echo of your yes.

When you live the More Life, you don't just leave memories; you leave momentum.

A woman who lives in surrender leaves ripples long after she's gone. Her prayers still work in the soil of her children's hearts. Her faith still speaks when her voice is silent.

When your dash is complete and your mist has cleared, may heaven echo over your life:

"Well done!"

And may those who follow you find courage in your example and faith in your footprints.

The question still lingers—no longer a whisper, but a holy call: *How will you be remembered?*

Selah: Remembered by Heaven

"The memory of the righteous is blessed" (Proverbs 10:7 NKJV).

There are sacred moments when God invites us to pause, not just to look back, but to look ahead. Legacy isn't written someday; it's being lived right now. Every yes, every act of faith, every unseen seed is a testimony that heaven remembers.

Take a deep breath. Breathe in gratitude. You are leaving fingerprints on eternity even now.

Pause & Reflect

- What "yes" is God asking of me right now that could shape my legacy?
- When others speak of me one day, what do I want them to say about my faith and love?
- Who am I pouring into (e.g., children, friends, mentees) so my legacy multiplies?
- What broken places in me is God filling with gold for the sake of others?
- If my life is a dash, how do I want to spend it?

Write honestly. Pray deeply. Let His presence steady you as you reflect.

Prayer of Legacy

Lord, teach me to number my days.

Let me not waste the mist, the dash, the thread You've given me.

Take every yes I've spoken, and every yes I still need to speak

and weave them into a story that glorifies You.

Fill my cracks with gold. Make my scars shine as testimonies.

Let my life outlast me by pointing others to You, the God of More.

May my legacy be faith, love, courage, and the fullness of Christ in me.

Amen.

Action Step: A Living Legacy Letter
Take time this week to write a short "legacy letter" to someone who matters deeply to you, perhaps a child, mentee, or friend. Share a lesson God has taught you, a prayer for their future, and a reminder of His faithfulness. Seal it, date it, and keep a copy for yourself as a commitment to live each day as the legacy you want to leave.

EPILOGUE
Living the More Life

The threads of this book have woven together a journey: from identity to trust, from healing to vision, from community to legacy. As you've walked with me through these pages, you've probably felt the ache for More. Maybe you've recognized the whispers of doubt, the labels of pain, the scars of your story, or the places where you've waited too long at the edge of transformation.

Here is the truth: *You were always made for More.* Not more hustle. Not more striving. Not more of what drains you. But the *exceedingly, abundantly More* of Christ (see Ephesians 3:20).

The More Life is not for the extraordinary woman. It is for the ordinary woman who dares to believe in an extraordinary God. For the one who is weary yet willing, broken yet hopeful, hidden yet seen. For the woman who whispers, "Yes, Lord. I believe there's More in You, and I believe there's More in me because of You."

A New Beginning: Living the More Life

"Now to Him who is able to do immeasurably more than all we ask or imagine, according to His power that is at work within us" (Ephesians 3:20).

You've come to the end of these pages, but not the end of your story. The More Life doesn't stop here. It begins here.

You have walked through identity, trust, healing, vision, community, and legacy. You've paused, reflected, prayed, and perhaps even wept. But this journey is not meant to be read once and set aside; It is intended to be lived, day by day, step by step, choice by choice.

The invitation still stands: *Rise. Reflect. Remember. Rebuild.* Live the More Life God dreamed for you before you ever took your first breath.

Prayer of Commitment to the More Life

Lord Jesus, I hear Your call.

I believe You created me for the More Life: a life of faith, courage, love, and legacy.

Today, I say yes.

Yes, to leaving behind fear, shame, and excuses.

Yes, to pressing into Your presence.

Yes, to walking boldly in the purpose You designed for me.

Fill me with Your Spirit.

Open my eyes to see as You see.

Give me courage to rise, strength to persevere, and faith to believe again.

Let my life be a testimony of Your grace, a light for my generation, and a legacy for those who come after me.

From this day forward, I choose the More Life because You, Lord, are more than enough.

In Jesus' name, Amen.

Final Reflections

Selah is a sacred pause: a moment to let truth settle deep into your spirit and ask yourself:

- What has God awakened in me through this journey?
- What have I laid down, and what new thing is He asking me to pick up?
- Where is He calling me to expand—spiritually, emotionally, or relationally?
- Who am I becoming because of this encounter with His More?

You are no longer just reading a story; you are living one. You are a story God Himself is still writing through your obedience, your courage, and your faith. Every step you take in trust becomes another line in the testimony He's crafting from your life. Your story, surrendered to His authorship, will echo beyond this moment, inviting others to believe that they, too, were made for More.

Next Steps: Walking Out the More Life

Transformation is sustained through intentional rhythms. Here are several next steps you can take to live the More Life in practical, life-giving ways:

1. Life Mapping

Chart your journey so far. Create a visual map of your life's defining moments: highs, lows, turning points, and "yes" moments. Then, mark where you've seen God's hand at work, even in the unseen places. Write a prayer of gratitude for each season, asking the Lord to show you how those moments prepared you for your next chapter.

2. Purpose Planning

Refine your "why." Ask yourself: What breaks my heart? What stirs my passion? What do I love to build, nurture, or restore? Draft a purpose statement that reflects your God-given assignment. Revisit it often, especially when life feels ordinary

3. Gift Inventory

Discover the unique ways God has wired you for impact. You can take a spiritual gifts assessment or a personality inventory (such as S.H.A.P.E. or CliftonStrengths). Identify the environments where you come alive, and the people you are called to serve. Write a declaration: "I will use what's in my hand for the glory of God."

4. Story Mapping

Your testimony is your tool. Write key stories from your journey of faith: your pit moments, your healing, your yeses. Reflect on how God's presence carried you through each one. Ask: Who needs to hear this part of my story? and look for opportunities to share it.

5. Daily Rhythms of Renewal

Sustainable transformation happens through consistent devotion. Create a simple rhythm of Scripture → Silence → Surrender → Step each day. Read a verse, pause to listen, release what's heavy, and act on what you hear. Keep a More Life Prayer Journal to record daily gratitude, answered prayers, and reflections.

6. Join the More Life Movement

You were never meant to walk alone. Consider joining the More Life Movement, a growing sisterhood of women committed to walking in faith, love, and purpose. You can join the More Life Movement and receive devotional updates and coaching tools by visiting www.monabrawley.com.

Final Selah: A Closing Benediction

"And I am certain that God, who began the good work within you, will continue His work until it is finally finished on the day when Christ Jesus returns" (Philippians 1:6 NLT).

Pause here. Place your hand over your heart. Breathe in the grace of God and exhale every weight that no longer belongs. You are not who you were when you began these pages. You are being transformed: renewed in purpose, strengthened by faith, and awakened to legacy. Selah.

Let it sink in: You were made for More.

Now, go live it! One yes, one step, one surrendered day at a time.

APPENDIX
Notes & Works Cited

What Do I Do Now?
First Steps to Growing in Your New Life with Christ

1. Get a Bible
Choose a translation that's easy to understand (NIV, NLT, or CSB are great places to begin). This is God's Word to you—your anchor and your daily source of strength.

2. Start Reading in the Gospel of John
Begin your journey by getting to know Jesus through His words, His love, and His life. Read a little each day and ask, "Lord, what are You showing me?"

3. Join a Bible-Based Church
You were never meant to grow alone. Find a Christ-centered, Scripture-teaching community where you can learn, worship, and build relationships that strengthen your walk with God.

4. Get Baptized
Baptism is a beautiful, public declaration of the inward change God has begun in you. Talk with your church about taking this step. It's a powerful way to say, "I belong to Jesus."

5. Pray Daily—Talk to God About Everything
Prayer is simply conversation. Share your hopes, fears, questions, and gratitude. He hears you and He cares for you deeply.

6. Take One Step at a Time
Spiritual growth is a journey. Give yourself grace, stay consistent, and trust the Holy Spirit to guide you forward.

7. Tell Someone About Your Decision

Share your salvation story with a friend, family member, pastor, or mentor. Your "yes" to Jesus is worth celebrating—and your testimony may inspire someone else.

Scripture References
The Holy Bible

Scripture quotations marked KJV are from the King James Version.

Scripture quotations marked NIV are from The Holy Bible, New International Version, NIV®.

Copyright © 1973, 1978, 1984, 2011 by Biblica, Inc.™ Used by permission. All rights reserved worldwide.

Scripture quotations marked NKJV are from the New King James Version®. Copyright © 1982 by Thomas Nelson. Used by permission. All rights reserved.

Research & Data Sources

Barna Group "Pastors Share Top Reasons They've Considered Quitting Ministry in the Past Year," Barna Group, March 15, 2022. https://www.barna.com/research/pastors-quitting-ministry

Lifeway Research "Debunking the Myths: Ministry Burnout and Leaving the Ministry." Lifeway Research, July 15, 2023. https://research.lifeway.com/2023/07/15/debunking-the-myths-ministry-burnout-and-leaving-the-ministry

U.S. Department of Health and Human Services, Office of the Surgeon General "Our Epidemic of Loneliness and Isolation: The U.S. Surgeon General's Advisory on the Healing Effects of Social Connection and Community," 2023. https://www.hhs.gov/sites/default/files/surgeon-general-social-connection-advisory.pdf

Ministry & Pastoral Leadership

Ethics & Religious Liberty Commission (ERLC) "The Loneliness of the Pastor's Wife." ERLC, 2016. https://erlc.com/resource-library/articles/the-loneliness-of-the-pastors-wife

Hoover, Christine "What Pastors' Wives Wish You Knew," The Gospel Coalition, April 11, 2017. https://www.thegospelcoalition.org/article/what-pastors-wives-wish-you-knew

Hill, Megan "6 Things Elders' Wives Wish You Knew," The Gospel Coalition, April 1, 2021. https://www.thegospelcoalition.org/article/elders-wives

Wilson, Katherine "Pastors' Wives and Mental Health: The Unseen Burden of Ministry," *Scholars Crossing Journal of Faith and Leadership*, 2025. (forthcoming publication, referenced with permission)

Brawley, Don L., III, DSL *Unleash: The Power to Build the Future You Were Born For*, 2025. Personal reflections and ministry partnership stories used with permission.

Daniels, Marshawn, E. Daniels, M. E. (2022). *365 Days of Believing Bigger* (p. 74). DaySpring.

Innovation & Faith in Action

National Park Service George Washington Carver National Monument – Biography. National Park Service, updated 2023. https://www.nps.gov/people/george-washington-carver.htm

Kremer, Gary R. *George Washington Carver: In His Own Words*, University of Missouri Press, 1987.

Lemelson Center for the Study of Invention and Innovation, Smithsonian Institution "Lewis H. Latimer: Lighting the Way,"

National Museum of American History, updated 2023. https://invention.si.edu/lewis-h-latimer-lighting-way

Latimer House Museum "The Lewis H. Latimer House Museum History and Legacy," Flushing, NY, 2023. https://www.lewislatimerhouse.org

Coaching & Personal Development
Chand, Brenda, D.Min. *You Can Coach: The Practical Coaching Manual*, Dream Releaser Coaching, 2018. *The Professional Coaching Handbook*, Dream Releaser Coaching, 2018.

Meyer, Joyce *Battlefield of the Mind: Winning the Battle in Your Mind*, FaithWords, 2002.

Titus, Devi *The Table Experience: Discover the Joy of Connecting with Family and Friends*, Life Bridge Press, 2013.

Spiritual Formation & Legacy
Warren, Rick *The Purpose Driven Life: What on Earth Am I Here For?*, Zondervan, 2002. *The Purpose Driven Church*, Zondervan, 2005.

Note on Sources
Biblical accounts, personal reflections, and coaching insights are drawn from Scripture and the author's lived experience. Historical materials are sourced from publicly available, government-verified, or scholarly references. All links were verified active as of October 2025.

ACKNOWLEDGEMENTS AND THANK YOUS!

Thank You

First and always, I give all honor and gratitude to my Lord and Savior, **Jesus Christ**. You are the Author and Finisher of my faith, the source of every calling, and the reason for every step forward. Thank You for Your grace that sustains me, Your truth that anchors me, and Your love that continually awakens me for more. To You alone be the glory.

This book would not exist without the love, patience, and unwavering support of my family.

To my husband, **Don**, thank you for leading me into uncharted territories with faith and courage, and for inviting me into the great adventure of following Jesus wholeheartedly, side by side. You have loved our family and me well, anchored our home with strength and grace, and consistently encouraged me to become all that God has called me to be—never to shrink, never to settle, but to step forward in faith. Your belief in me has been a steady wind at my back.

To Dana, thank you for your steady support, your encouragement, and the way you continue to lift me with your love and presence. I am grateful to you.

To our children, **Brandon (Kristie-Love), Chantelle (Marquice), and Aaron (Adeline Joy)**, your prayers, your pride, and your encouragement have strengthened me throughout this process. Thank you for cheering me on and believing in the message God placed in my heart.

To **Aaron**, thank you for offering your writing expertise and thoughtful feedback. Your insight helped shape this work in meaningful ways.

To my grandchildren, **Isabella, Mila, Brandon, Bishop** and all the precious grands on the way, you are reminders of God's faithfulness and joy. You give me the courage and the motivation to live life to the full. I hope that one day you will read these words and know without question that you, too, were made for more.

To my **Impact Church family** and the **Women of Impact**, thank you for loving me, praying for me, and walking this journey with me. Serving and growing alongside you is one of the greatest honors of my life. You have made this season a dream.

Thank you all for walking this journey with me. Your love, support, and faith are woven into every page.

Dr. Mona L. Brawley is a pastor, educator, author, and coach with a heart for faith, family, and meaningful connection. She is married to Dr. Don Brawley III, and together they are the proud parents of three children and grandparents to a growing family circle.

Mona lives in the Atlanta, Georgia area, where she enjoys traveling, spending time in nature, creating unhurried moments with her children and grandchildren, and life with her two beloved dogs. She values thoughtful conversation, shared laughter, and walking alongside others as they discover the life they were created to live.

Connect at www.monabrawley.com